T0384286

The Old Jewish Men's Guide

to EATING, SLEEPING, AND FUTZING AROUND

The COMPLETE HANDBOOK
for Thriving in This Fakakta World

NOAH RINSKY · Illustrated by DICK CARROLL

WORKMAN PUBLISHING ◆ NEW YORK

WORKMAN
Workman Publishing
Hachette Book Group, Inc.
1290 Avenue of the Americas
New York, NY 10104
workman.com

Workman is an imprint of Workman Publishing,
a division of Hachette Book Group, Inc.
The Workman name and logo are registered trademarks
of Hachette Book Group, Inc.

Design by RAPHAEL GERONI

Workman books may be purchased in bulk for business, educational, or promotional use.
For information, please contact your local bookseller or the Hachette Book Group
Special Markets Department at special.markets@hbgusa.com.

Names: Rinsky, Noah, author.
Title: The old Jewish men's guide to eating, sleeping, and futzing around : the complete
handbook for how to thrive in this fakata world / Noah Rinsky ; illustrated by Dick Carroll.
Description: First edition. | New York : Workman Publishing, 2024. |
Identifiers: LCCN 2024002430 (print) | LCCN 2024002431 (ebook) | ISBN 9781523523566 |
ISBN 9781523523573 (epub)
Subjects: LCSH: Jews—Humor. | Men—Humor. | Jewish wit and humor.
Classification: LCC PN6231.J5 R56 2024 (print) | LCC PN6231.J5 (ebook) | DDC
808.88/2—dc23/eng/20240326
LC record available at https://lccn.loc.gov/2024002430
LC ebook record available at https://lccn.loc.gov/2024002431
ISBN 978-1-5235-2356-6

First Edition September 2024

Printed in China on responsibly sourced paper.

10 9 8 7 6 5 4 3 2 1

CONTENTS

PRE(R)AMBLE

OVER THE YEARS, MY SECRETARY HAS RECEIVED countless messages—I've even read a few of them!—from young, passionate fans from all over the world who want to know how to become Old Jewish Men. Oy gevalt! The truth is, it's no walk in the park. Performing endoscopic sinus surgery? No problem. Landing an aircraft after six martinis? Have at it. Building a coalition in the Knesset? Piece of cake.

But being an Old Jewish Man is hard.

This is a lifestyle acquired through years of dedicated practice. It's like feeling your way to the refrigerator with the lights off, or knowing exactly what constitutes South Florida cardigan weather. It's a map from deep within—pure instinct, baby. Ten thousand hours? Pfft. Try a lifetime. Take, for instance, the time your wife asked you to clean out the bathtub, so you called the guy—it's difficult to teach that kind of expertise.

But make no mistake: The ways of an OJM *can* be learned. By reading this book and applying its principles to everyday life, you will not only be able to sniff out the best wonton soup in your city with precision, know the right sandals to wear to your accountant's funeral, and pick the least expired tub of cottage cheese, but you will also begin to mature—with varying degrees of class—into your final form.

Soon enough, you'll be smoking a hand-rolled Partagas, combing your hairpiece, and whining about the Mets while your Turkish tailor lets three inches out of your cabana slacks. You'll absorb valuable information: the best bench to sit on in Seward Park, which urethra clamp to purchase after your prostate surgery, and the top-rated urinal to use at the Transit Museum (if you can make it there in time). Pinpointing the primo place to fall asleep at your niece's wedding will become second nature, like passing gas on public transportation.

Remember, OJM is a lifestyle, and you don't even have to be old or Jewish or a man . . . but it sure doesn't hurt. So, when you get to the end of this book and ask yourself, *Why did I waste my time reading that? Does Barnes & Noble allow people to return products that have been thrown against the wall?*, you will realize that my writing a half-assed tome is all part of the grift . . . uh, I mean the *lifestyle*.

The bottom line is that I have devoted my life to learning the ways of the Old Jewish Man, and, despite being in my thirties, I am one. I started this whole thing because I missed my old Jewish dad (and my mom—hi, Mom, I didn't forget about you!) who moved to Tel Aviv in 2012, and I didn't have anyone around offering to make me kasha every eight minutes. I'm a proud Jew, and my love for Judaism extends beyond bagels and delis and chest hair and the shvitz and funny accents, though it does include those things.

For those who feel like they can relate to OJM or are reminded of someone they love in these pages, that's the point. For anyone offended, well, you already paid me. Thank you to my seventy-and-over club (more in the Acknowledgments) for showing me the way. Because of you my waistband is right where it's supposed to be: just below my nipples.

—Noah Rinsky

NYPL, *Schwarzman Building*
NEW YORK CITY
Feb. 2024

Greater OJM Pecking Order

HEAD CHIEF MACHER

This guy always gets the best seat.

Don't skimp on the whitefish, and more napkins next time. Who ate all the kippered herring?!

DIRECTOR OF THE GREATER SPREAD

EXECUTIVE BIG MACHER TO THE BIG SHOT

New York President of Picking Out the Most Comfortable Used Office Chairs

Head of Kasha Risk Management aka Throwing Kasha to the Wind

Head of "I Don't Tip on Bad Service"

Manager of Finding the Lunch Spot that Includes Tax in the Prices and Has Free Pickles

President of Herring, Onions, Caviar, and Frozen Vodka Department

Minister of "Leave Me the Hell Alone When I'm Reading the Newspaper"

Secretary of Sneaking Out of Shul Early

Director of "Don't Forget to Bring a Sweater to South Florida"

President of "The Water Pressure Here Is No Good"

Assistant to the Chief of Buying Up All the High Holiday Aliyahs

Chief Bagel and Bialy Hole Inspector

Vice President of the Double Collar/ Cardigan Combination

Big Tuna of the Tuna and Other Salty Fish

COMPLAINTS DEPT. CHIEF

Continues on other side!

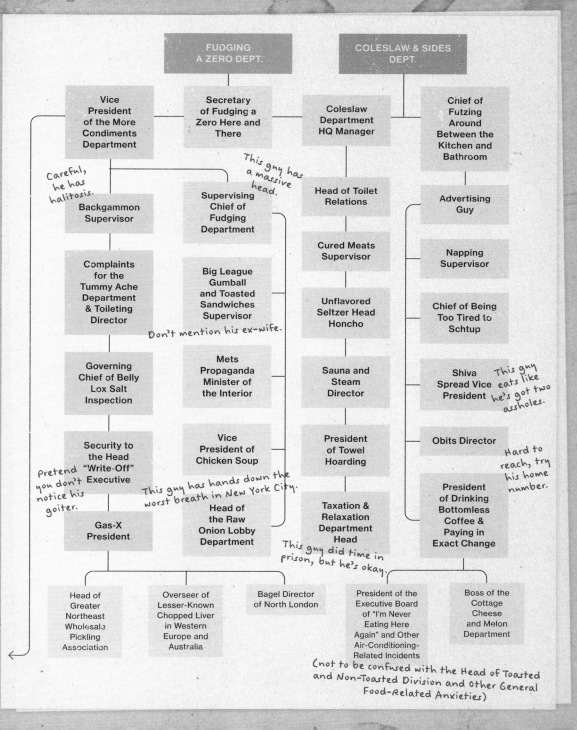

The  DICTIONARY

An ask: a favor that is requested of an OJM that requires moving or schlepping. According to Reb Velvel Osofsky of Zonsky, in the time of Exodus, around 1440 BCE, Moses reportedly shrugged when G-d commanded him to take the Jews out of Egypt. "This is quite the ask," he was heard to grumble.

Cheating: euphemism for eating everything on the menu at a deli, usually after receiving a questionable bill of health.

Crumbing: knowingly having crumbs or filth around the mouth and refusing to clean them out of spite.

First futz: a morning walking ritual that comes either directly before the first cup of coffee or directly after.

Free roll: when someone else is paying. Ex: *"We're free rolling on Avi today, fellas. So eat for two!"*

Give me ten: announcement prior to a bathroom visit.

Going on a date: visiting the proctologist.

Having a cigar with Moses: euphemism for saying someone died.

Hay allergy: code for not wanting to go somewhere because there will be a person, usually another OJM, whom you don't like.
Ex: *"I'd come but my hay allergy is acting up."*

(Jewish) lightning: a fire that is deliberately started in a building or property for the insurance money. Etymologists say the joke came from the famous Brownsville fire of 1922, in which Mickey Tooberman was implicated: "Sorry about your house burning down, Mickey." *"Shhhhh!* It's tomorrow."

Long goodbye: code for when an Old Jewish Man's wife takes forever to say goodbye to everyone at a party. Ex: *"Here we go, here comes the long goodbye."*

Oil change: going to the doctor; can also mean going in for surgery.

Peared: connoting an OJM body shape resembling a pear.

Pedal weather: a forecast that suggests perfect bicycle conditions. No rain, no sleet, no ice, no snow, no nothin'. Smooth sailing.

Power doughnut: the fine strip of hair around both sides of a bald head.

Pulling out: the act of removing yourself from an unsavory conversation.

Sittery: a place, usually a restaurant, that is a good spot to sit and where the waiters leave you alone.

Sleeping on fresh sheets: having a clean bill of health.

Slow morning: code for being constipated.

Sopper: of or relating to bread. Certain breads transform into a sopping agent, as they contact liquid. The English muffin, for instance, is a good vehicle for sopping up egg yolk. Ex: *"Get to work, Lester. You got two soppers and a pool of yolk on your plate."*

Steamrolling: the act of continuing to talk, but at a higher volume, while somebody else interrupts, asks a question, or challenges an Old Jewish Man's opinion on anything.

Suckers: people who wait in line.

Taking a meeting: code for having a bowel movement. Scholars contend the phrase was carried over from Verkhnyadzvinsk, Belarus, around 1890.

Throne: code for toilet, belonging to a vernacular originating on West 78th Street and Columbus Avenue. Currently a pointed term referring to one's own need to walk to their home john. It's thought to have once been a derisive statement referring to the lack of public lavatories on the Upper West Side of Manhattan.

Toileting: the act of using the toilet.

Tuchus-watcher: an Old Jewish Man whose only interest in going to the beach is to look at butts.

Zayde wad: the mandatory cash roll that an Old Jewish Man must have on him at all times. The big bill (a fifty or a hundred) always goes on the outside, and the one-dollar bills go in the center.

The BASICS

THE BEAUTY OF BECOMING an OJM is that there's zero intention behind it. It's not the path of least resistance—it's barely even a path. This is a slow, uncalculated shuffle toward an incidental life stage that can be summed up best by a few factors. For instance, you: take your hot dog with mustard and kraut, urinate an excessive amount at Citi Field, remain close friends with your divorce attorney, hate to travel, take your meetings in the shvitz, study the bond yield curve every day, have reread *Master of the Senate* (unabridged), smoke cigars, dry your own kosher salami, drive a Cadillac, enjoy talking about your body with strangers, refuse to wear sunscreen, stare at people, eat grilled salmon more than once a week, are addicted to buying German sports cars, eat at JG Melon, go to the doctor more often than you go to the grocery store, chew with your mouth open, snore, always carry a handkerchief, dine at luncheonettes, live on the Lower East Side, take the bus, give strangers unsolicited advice, harbor a strong dislike of nature, own multiple failing businesses, wear a Rolex, can't spell, think diet and exercise is a myth, own more than twenty pairs of loafers, have never figured out chopsticks, keep three pairs of glasses hanging on your shirt, refuse to wear socks, nap all the time, never ask for directions, live to give directions, are terrified of driving, run red lights, collect batteries, are afraid of sushi, carry a pocket calculator, puke on airplanes, call waiters "WAITER!", drink smoothies, refuse to wear jeans, gamble on sports, have been married to your third cousin for sixty-eight years, hate dogs, collect stamps, get frequent haircuts, tip everyone in cash, wear a pinky ring, wear a toupee, play billiards, live in South Florida, have spent years trying to corner the grave plot market, wear New Balance 608v5s, have been pinched for your work as a bookie, have a penicillin allergy, don't eat pork, are prone to rashes, have always had a mustache, refuse hearing aids, refuse to talk on the phone, wear slippers outside, only drink Vintage seltzer, sleep in the sauna, nibble Entenmann's crumb cake in the sauna, booze in the sauna, snore through weddings, eat chips on the golf course, pay $430 for a rent-stabilized apartment on the Upper West Side, are personal friends with Stanley and Saul Zabar, breathe through your mouth, don't realize you have cataracts, can't park without crashing, have never left New York except that one time you visited Florida and went to the hospital for a sunburn, think the FBI is listening to your conversations with the lox slicer, hang out in libraries, hang out on park benches, can't stand being outside, believe talking is yelling and yelling is talking, haven't spoken to your wife in a decade, don't know what day it is, maintain that nitrates are a conspiracy, play chess, play poker, play gin, stuff your pockets with condiment packets, hoard napkins, sell rugs, keep a bag of unpaid parking tickets, get plastic surgery, own a jet, have a lifelong mistress who's now a senior citizen, keep a list of people who have spurned you, and don't consider yourself old.

||||||||||||||||||||||

These basics offer a glimpse of the sorts of Old Jewish Men futzing around out there in the world. OJM can—with zero exceptions and no nuance—fit into ten taxonomic categories, which we'll sprinkle throughout the book (turn the page for our first one). No more, no less-ish. Oh sure, we can argue about it all day, but who has the energy?

>   INVISIBLE   ⋯⋯⋯>   *Repulsive*   ⋯⋯⋯>   ꒰ꗃꗃꗃ꒱ CUTE

New York Schlubs

> "In no other city can a total schlub also be an absolute success."

—AARON COHEN
Midwood resident, age unknown, retired stain identification expert

Crumbs, sauce stains, and pants hiked up to their nipples—these are the hallowed OJM Schlubs of the tristate. They wear nice long-sleeve collared shirts that their wives pick out from Brooks Brothers but soil them immediately with mustard drippings, coffee runoff, and Zabar's latke grease. Unbeknownst to Schlubs, their sneakers have been untied for the last ten years, and today is finally the day they get dragged to Harry's Shoes for a new Velcro pair. "Fine, FINE, I'll go!" they shout. These guys are the wide-waisted, pants-over-the-shoes public defenders whose minds have grown completely disconnected from their bodies. Sartorial savants, some say.

New York Schlubs are sedentary intellectuals who have succumbed to a deeper, arguably spiritual state that can only be described as "being there." They sit in recliners sucking down Popsicles while reading detective books and bingeing summer sports.

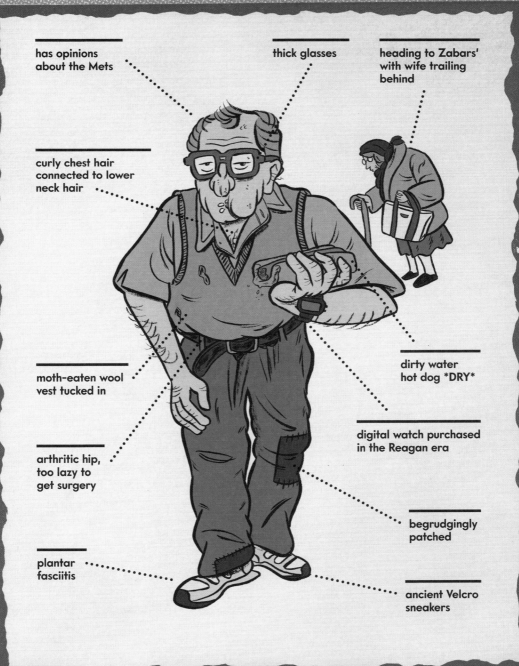

has opinions about the Mets

thick glasses

heading to Zabars' with wife trailing behind

curly chest hair connected to lower neck hair

moth-eaten wool vest tucked in

arthritic hip, too lazy to get surgery

plantar fasciitis

dirty water hot dog *DRY*

digital watch purchased in the Reagan era

begrudgingly patched

ancient Velcro sneakers

They have a knack for starting conversations somewhere in the middle, and their self-esteem is rock solid, wearing their finger eczema like a badge of honor.

These men are medical miracles. They can remain utterly inert, living on cream cheese bagels, wontons, spoonfuls of chocolate sprinkles, and Benazepril. They're saddled with high blood pressure and prostates the size of grapefruits, yet they live to ninety-four. When there's some health hiccup (like a ping pong ball–size anal goiter) or an irregularity that becomes too obvious to ignore, their doctors (who also happen to be lifelong friends) shrug and make them promise to cut down the beef lo mein to once a week. These fellas always nod their heads in agreement and then beeline it to the nearest hot dog stand. One dog is never enough, and sauerkraut is basically a salad.

Monologuin'

It may surprise you to learn that, despite their neglectful appearance, many New York Schlubs are major success stories. If you ever find yourself chatting with one—bring an absorbent rag for any spittle hurled at your forehead—you may slowly glean from his rambling that he made a fortune doing unconventional things like opening chess schools in Belarus, wholesaling piano strings, arbitraging whiskey barrels and horsehair, and negotiating buyouts and sellouts and leveraging them into lawsuits while shorting Japanese talking toilet companies. You know, business. You may also learn that these fellas know just about everything about New York City. They're walking tour guides who monologue like they're on talk radio. You can turn these fellas on, but good luck turning 'em off.

Masters of the Blab

A Schlub's voice has a lulling quality that both bores and entices you into giving up whatever goals you once had in a conversation that has lost any trace of a through line. Ten minutes in and he's somehow hypnotized you with presidential trivia about which you know nothing: *Calvin Coolidge was the only commander in chief born on the Fourth of July.* Yet through it all, these New York Schlubs keep us coming back. They're endless, bottomless, barrel-shaped receptacles of surprisingly stimulating, albeit useless, facts that give way to entirely new curiosities we never knew we had.

OBIT by ARI EPSTEIN WEINRAUB,
National JCC Bulletin

MR. NEW YORK SCHLUB,

whose diet from adolescence to senility consisted of cream cheese, stadium dogs, untoasted buttered kaiser rolls, corned beef, and gumballs, died at the age of 104, outliving one of the nurses assigned to his hospice care in the 1990s. His great-granddaughter declined to provide a cause of death, saying that the true nature of Mr. Schlub's health was impossible to determine. He claimed to suffer from ailments including diabetes, heart arrhythmia, and dementia, yet became mysteriously vigorous and lucid watching Mets games and critiquing Mrs. Schlub's cooking.

2 HOT DOG RECIPES

"Two words: raw onions. White, not red. Mustard."

—*Lewis Brown*, 97, lifelong New Yorker

"Better be an all-beef dog. One line of mustard—NO ketchup. Peppers, tomato wedges, onion, pickle, celery salt. Steamed bun."

—*Gussy Yusselman*, 100, lifelong Chicago (and honorary NY) Schlub

"Leaving home isn't advisable,
but if you have to, make sure
there's a half-decent spread."

—*Kafka*, most likely

CHAPTER 1

How to Exist in This Fakakta World

Old Jewish Men don't ever seem to go anywhere, and yet they have a habit of inexplicably materializing everywhere. Whether they're snoring front row at the US Open, sending back food at the Blue Note, plugging their ears at some high-profile fashion show, yawning through the Oscars, or annihilating Cracker Jacks on the Citi Field jumbotron, their mere presence will appear strange and effortless. "Why is he here?" onlookers will ask.

The answer is that OJM gotta exist in this fakakta world, same as everybody else. From baseball watching to using a spiffy museum commode to hearing a little jazz at the club, this is your guide to enjoying yourself outside the house—even when your body language conveys dissatisfaction, mild confusion, and, above all, condescension to the willing parties around you who paid full ticket price.

Scuffin' It Up on the Diamond

ENJOYING OUR NATIONAL pastime means nine solid innings of napping, eating, toileting, and rattling off a long string of useless facts loosely related to rosters, managerial decisions, batting averages, condiment prices, and outrageous theories about polyester-to-cotton uniform ratios, all with little to no accuracy. Who cares if what you're saying has any basis in reality? Or if anyone is even listening? Because when it comes down to it, there's nothing better than the sound of your own voice. (Although catching a cab in midtown during rush hour comes pretty close.)

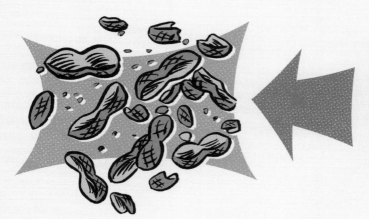

Don't leave the stadium without amassing a gigantic mound of shells from nine innings of snacking.

It's not a day at the ball game without it.

When in Doubt, Talk Louder

If some meddler in the seat next to you disputes your baseball theories, it's basic conversational procedure to never acknowledge his or anyone else's opinion, knowledge, or physical presence. After all, an Old Jewish Man is the expert on everything if he so chooses. Alternatively, you may simply steamroll them by making the same point ad infinitum, but at a much louder volume—that usually does the trick.

Sitting next to an actual smart person at a game—whether they're well-studied in science, math, history, politics, or sports—is a nightmare scenario for your OJM viewing experience. Instead, surround yourself with dimmer bulbs who will laugh at all your jokes and be interested in your stories. The less they know, the more guffaws you'll get, which is the most important thing. Catching an afternoon ball game is all about eating a lot, cracking jokes, and stuffing your pockets with free condiment packets. Hopefully the Mets get a win, too.

OJM SPORTSBOOK

SPORTING EVENT OVER/UNDERS

No sporting event is worth your attention without some sort of wager. Put some skin in the game—otherwise you might as well be doing something useful, like picketing the rising price of cantaloupe.

O/U 33 trips to the boys' room

O/U 19 frankfurters

O/U 5 ice cream cones

O/U 60 cups of water

O/U 8,000 yawns

O/U 500 nose blows

O/U 120 crotch adjustments

**GO-TO
BASEBALL
SNACKS TO
SMUGGLE
FROM
HOME**

**CRACKER
JACKS**

◆

**WHOLE
PEANUTS**

◆

**TWO-LITER
RC COLA**

◆

**JUNIOR
MINTS**

◆

**CLAUSSEN
PICKLES**

◆

**ZIPLOCK BAG
of HOMEMADE
SAUERKRAUT**

Advanced Koufax Trivia 501

At times you may find yourself wondering if you've already said this or that before. For the love of Lipitor, ignore that ridiculous feeling and continue your pointless tirade. Baseball games are a great place to kick back and tell thirty versions of the same story you've been repeating over the last several decades. A little-known gem like "Sandy Koufax was a better basketball player than a baseball player" is both a keeper to use constantly and great supplemental material for the Classic Koufax Anecdote. Every OJM knows that Sandy didn't pitch on Yom Kippur, so spice up the spiel once in a while. (What your captive interlocutor *won't* know is that Dandy Sandy's replacement that day, Don Drysdale, pitched the worst inning of his life, was taken out, and reportedly told Dodgers manager Walter Alston after the game, "Hey, Skip, bet you wish I was Jewish today, too." That story is a gift that will keep on giving.)

The Raw Onion Crisis

Forget supply chains, inflation, climate change, and all the other noise you hear on CNN. Ever since the pandemic, the disgraceful removal of raw onions at our nation's ballparks has reached crisis levels. Don't be mistaken, baseball teams are not the victims of this condiment emergency—you are. You can bet your ass that the big shots upstairs in the boxes have got buckets of raw bulbs to dice and dump on their dogs. Buckets! It's always the little guys in the trenches who end up treading water with weights on their feet, eating bare, onion-less wieners.

So whether you're at Game 7 of the World Series or spring training in Fort Myers, do your part in the fight and make a scene about the lack of raw onions. Make sure to scream at the tired low-wage worker cramming your boiled frank into a flavorless bun: "How the hell am I supposed to eat this?!"

FIVE GRUMPIEST OJM OWNERS IN SPORTS

1. **ARTHUR BLANK:** Your team blowing a 28–3 lead in the Super Bowl is more than enough to make you a little grumpy. The Falcons have stunk ever since.

2. **DARYL KATZ:** You'd be pretty irritable too if you were also battling a life-threatening sinus infection like this Oilers owner. No kidding. Get better soon, Daryl.

3. **MARK DAVIS:** A sub-.400 winning percentage as a Raiders owner shows room for improvement. We miss Al Davis.

4. **MARK CUBAN:** Can't blame you for being grumpy, Mark. You haven't won much since Dirk and it's unclear whether this Luka character will ever take the Mavs back to the promised land.

5. **BOB KRAFT:** Bob's a little crotchety, but he's a billionaire sitting on six Patriot Super Bowl rings with a great-looking doctor wife thirty-three years his junior. Be like Bob.

"Old Jewish Men don't like the Yankees. The Yankees are Wall Street. The Mets are the underdogs, just like us."

—*Jules Coleman,* Sheepshead Bay, 75, retired Yale law professor and total baseball crank

Keepers of the Phlegm

According to the OJM Baseball Facts and Statistics Bureau, Major League Baseball has had it in for Old Jewish Men for a long time. It sure was suspicious when the league suddenly decided that "there's no place for the spitball," the secret phlegmy pitch that players like Erskine Mayer, a highly congested chronic nose blower, needed to strike out batters. Other all-time OJM pitching greats like Marv Rotblatt, who apparently produced a lot of natural phlegm, complained that it wasn't fair to strip him of his only natural evolutionary advantage. Even worse, those uptight MLB stiffs ruled that not only are you barred from hocking a loogie into your hand, but you can't even call in a pinch spitter to do the job for you. What a shonda.

The Stink of Ebbets

You have a solemn responsibility to speak of Ebbets Field in elegiac tones whenever anyone mentions the Dodgers. Names like Koufax, Robinson, Reese, and Hodges should always remain on the tip of your tongue, and any trip to Brooklyn will be interrupted by an extensive, detour to the old Ebbets Field grounds on Empire Boulevard. This is where you can drive around the block for several hours delivering vital pieces of information, such as "Did you know that the left side of the supermarket is exactly where the pitching mound used to be?"

If and when you have grandkids of your own, it's your duty to raise dedicated Mets or Dodgers fans. Educating the little ones on the history of baseball is no small undertaking: Try fun, kid-friendly activities like explaining in excruciating detail why the New York Giants were never much of a ball club and Bobby Thomson was a sign-stealing bum. And tell everyone you know that no matter how many pennants a team has won or how good their concession choices are, there will never again be *anything* quite like the Brooklyn Dodgers. What a shame that they'll never get to see it—at least you still get to blab about it.

These Seats Are No Good

The best part about taking the 7 Train to Citi Field is you won't worry about the price of gas or parking. The worst part? Sitting next to your sweaty cousin Seymour. Don't forget to bring binoculars, sunscreen, a suitcase packed with snacks from home, a tuchus cushion, Tylenol, coffee, sugar cookies, and a cold Vintage seltzer. Old Jewish Men don't sit in the nosebleeds—whine to the usher about your back problems until they give you a better seat for the same price. Don't think twice about letting people know that your body is falling apart and threaten to sue the stadium for not having enough water fountains. Pity is a weapon, and the world is here to accommodate your every demand. When in doubt, be litigious.

DAVE'S BASEBALL GAME VALUE HACK

shifty eyes, great for finding value

hairline that starts at the middle of the head

huge ears clogged with follicle mounds

tan, hard skin from falling asleep on the beach in Far Rockaway

trademark mustache

Not only does OJM Superstar Dave Roffe keep kosher, but he also refuses to pay stadium concession prices (shocking). He explains: "I usually take a bag of dried kosher salami from home in a ziplock bag. They never check your pockets. Then, when I get to the stadium, they'll give me a hamburger bun for a dime. I use all their free condiments and have the best kosher sandwich in the house, and I save thirty bucks."

Too Hot. I'm Thirsty.

Thirst should be quenched with a giant cup of seltzer from an ancient, oversized plastic memorabilia cup, but make sure they "go easy on the ice!" and give you free refills. If anyone dares deny you a seltzer top off, immediately launch into a rant about getting "no respect" while grabbing heaping handfuls of condiment packets to stuff in your pockets for future use. You never know—today it's the raw onions, tomorrow it's the relish. Stay vigilant.

100%

The amount of OJM who would run over their own mother to see the Mets finish the season with a better record than the Yanks.

Own Your Dome

The next time you're at Citi Field or Dodger Stadium, take your hand out of your pants and look around. You'll be sure to see quite a few bald Old Jewish Men with exposed heads. Why don't these fellas wear hats? As you earn your stripes within the organization, you'll understand that OJM go places to *show off* their shiny domes—the orb itself is a symbol of power and beauty. There's nothing sexier than a tan power doughnut, and bitching incessantly about being bald is the oldest trick in the book. It's like complaining about being a millionaire.

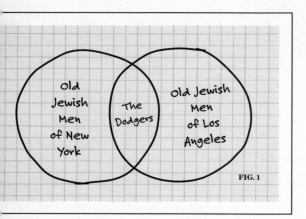

There've been lots of well-respected fellas over the years who, for whatever reason, fought against balding by embracing the toupee. Many were justified in their decision, but you're not there yet.

8

Word to the wise: Don't be the guy asking his wife to brush out his fox hair head-rug before bed. Mow the middle and keep the sides, fella—this is the way. We love you, Jackie Mason (RIP), but everyone knew you were bald seven decades ago. You too, George Burns. Wear your doughnut to the ball game proudly.

head wart that needs to be removed

huge ears

furrowed brow from years of contemplating mortality

perfectly shaped power doughnut

recently trimmed side hair

QUIZ: WHAT KIND OF BALD JEW ARE YOU?

☐ Hat ☑ No hat

☑ Power doughnut ☐ Completely bald

☑ Glasses ☐ Contacts

☐ Beard ☑ Clean-shaven

C O N G R A T U L A T I O N S !
You were born in Sheepshead Bay in 1947, wrote a string of successful sitcoms, and now own a $20 million house in Brentwood.

THE UNSUNG BENEFITS OF
Baldness

by LIANA SATENSTEIN, fashion writer

WITH BALD MEN, you know what you're getting, whether they're shedding prematurely or at a ripe old age. It's the signature hairstyle of honesty. There's nothing to hide. That should be a great thing, and yet, hair loss has been demonized by society. But why? Baldness is like baring one's soul, but on your head. There are no hair plugs, no follicle transplants, no toupees, no spray-ons, and no biotin lotions. Instead, you got one beautiful shining orb to show off: naked, undressed, and ready for a good rub.

Plus, baldness and hunkiness go hand in hand. There are the brooding babes like Jason Statham, Bruce Willis, and Shemar Moore. They look like testosterone ever so easily emanates from their depilated pores. It's hot, even sensual.

But that's just the physical appeal of baldness, the tip of the glabrous iceberg. The brashness of baldness connects to the soul, to the brain. Take the Larry David types with a power doughnut, a look that consists of two swaths of hair hanging on for dear life. Why not shave it all off? Why not cover the spot with *something*? Jesus, anything. Because the P.D. is a power move. It's the unbridled crop circle of self-awareness that results in confidence and wit. *Delicious.*

So, whether you're leaning into brolic full baldness or a bold power doughnut, keep the pattern of male pattern baldness going. In fact, lean into it. Be bald, be sexy, and most of all, be you—but hairless.

KICKIN' IT COURTSIDE

APPRECIATION FOR basketball starts young, around the time Old Jewish Men get cut from their junior high teams for being too short and criticizing the game plan too loudly. Even if they're lucky enough to play through their high school and college years, they soon realize that there's nowhere to go but sideways—to the coaching staff on the bench. As natural obsessives, statisticians, and speculators, clipboard holding and complaining to referees comes naturally. Don't forget, all-time alte kaker coaches Red Auerbach and Red Holzman were OJM. (And fun fact: The first official NBA basket was scored by Knicks guard and future OJM Ossie Schectman on November 1, 1946.) There's nothing like getting the blood pressure up while arguing about preseason games decades after they've finished. Remember: In sports, the coach who yells the loudest wins.

Parking Is a Hassle

Transportation-wise, going to a basketball game is a whole different animal compared to baseball. For one thing, hoops season is during the winter, so guess what? It's cold. For another, there's lousy parking at Barclays Center, and don't let anyone tell you differently. The arena lies at the center point of one of the most ghastly, congested intersections in Brooklyn, where there's enough traffic fumes for you to contract an inoperable lung tumor before you find your seat. And if you're walking there from 7th Avenue Donuts—more than a likelihood—you'd think you fell into a manhole and woke up in Des Moines. Good thing they cleared out an entire neighborhood just to stick a terrible shopping center right next to the ugliest basketball arena in the country. No championship, no mercy.

MR. WHAMMY, THE SUPERFAN SOUL OF THE NETS

Old Jewish Men don't root for the Nets—they cheer for octogenarian Brooklyn native Bruce Reznick, aka Mr. Whammy. Bruce bought season tickets twenty-six years ago and has been "putting the whammy" on opposing players ever since. What does it mean to whammy? He hexes the visiting team's free throw shooters with varying degrees of taunts. It works, too—just ask Shaq. One rule: Reznick never whammies ex-Nets players. You gotta have principles in life, and if people don't like them, have other ones ready to go. So if you're gonna trudge up Flatbush Avenue to Barclays, go for Bruce.

great hairline

powerful voice box

impeccable pointer finger

The Art of Beating Stadium Traffic

The desire to not get road-clogged is up there with eating, having short and efficient intercourse, owning a bigger house than your cousin Gussy, and sitting naked in a hot, moist room for hours with nothing but Phil Schaap purring on the radio. Time is of the essence, and in this stage of your life, don't wait for anything. Gridlock is for suckers, so master the back roads to ensure it doesn't happen to you. An easy rule to live by: If a team is down seven points at any part of the fourth quarter, this is your cue to get up and beat traffic. If they come back, you'll catch it on FM.

It's crucial to prioritize saving five minutes in the car over almost anything, no matter how mad family and friends get at you for leaving early. This goes far beyond the ball game—you should be ready to jump ship abruptly during urology appointments, your third favorite granddaughter's wedding, Little League championships, five-card stud, shofar blowing, megillah readings, fishing trips with your wife's brother (what a bore), sitting shiva, jury duty, root canals, personal training sessions, a bris, CT scans, and mid-coitus ("Sorry, sweetheart, papa's gotta boogie.") However: An Old Jewish Man never *ever* leaves the golf course early for any reason.

HIGH ABOVE COURTSIDE: REMEMBERING BOSTON CELTICS ANNOUNCER JOHNNY MOST

OJM broadcasting legend Johnny Most had nicknames for everyone he didn't think was playing the game right (or plain didn't like). Magic Johnson was "Cry-Baby Johnson"—*"Cry-Baby with the turnaround three!"* Washington Bullets players Rick Mahorn and Jeff Ruland were "McFilthy" and "McNasty." He loved to criticize the horrible, dirty "Bad Boy" Detroit Pistons. He called Bill Laimbeer "Counterfeit Bill" and Isiah Thomas "Little Lord Fauntleroy." Johnny was tougher than a two-dollar steak and continued calling games and smoking two packs a day even after he had his legs amputated—a true OJM right to the end.

Jack and Lou

Honorary OJM Jack Nicholson is the master of
screaming at referees from a seated position.
When the Lakers are getting spanked, count on
Nicholson yelling between bites of a salty dog,
gesticulating aggressively with the end of a
soggy bun. If you're rich enough to watch
the game in high-def, you can spot the globs
of mustard caked to the Jack-Man's lip as
shards of raw onion fly out of his open
mouth. Jack embodies a slovenly, masculine caliber of OJM that is at once
completely at ease, utterly present, and nearly impossible to attain. Good luck trying.

Lou Adler is a lot more than just the OJM who sits next to Jack. He's a record
producer in the Rock & Roll Hall of Fame who signed bands like The Mamas &
the Papas and was responsible for all-time hits like "California Dreamin'" and
"Monday, Monday." If Lou's not watching the action with Jack or a great-lookin'
gal, he brings his son. The Greater OJM Community encourages members to
spend time with offspring, but only if the kids are mensches. So what to do if
your kid looks and acts like a putz? This is the question many an OJM must
grapple with, as Jewish men don't hit their stride until their late seventies. OJM
guidelines recommend making these young guns get a haircut and pull their
pants up to their sternums.

Bringing Your Hot Gentile Wife to the Game

What's the point of marrying a fantastic lookin' gentile if you
don't bring her absolutely everywhere? OJM like Michael
Douglas, Philip Roth, Larry King, and newlywed Larry David
have paraded their non-Jewish wives and girlfriends around
like it's a new kidney. With the familial grief that can
sometimes come from intermarriage, these fellas wanna
get their anguish-worth-of-kicks by wedding women with
names like Ashley Underwood, Claire Johnson, and
Margaret Martinson. And so should you!

THERE ARE FEW GREATER JOYS in life than marrying a gentile. Larry King loved it so much he did it at least a half-dozen times. Take it from me—every day feels like I'm George Bailey waking up on Christmas surrounded by shellfish and foreskins. I proudly dote on my children, safe in the knowledge that thanks to their mother, they aren't relegated to being simple podiatrists or estate attorneys. They can also be politicians, parking valets, even serial killers.

Some may wonder, "How can I ensure my heritage and culture are represented?" Friend, I am proud to report that there are many varieties of gentile who also feel paralyzing pangs of guilt, shout through most meals, and enjoy gold chains. Even if your spouse does not come from a Culture of Kvetching, that in and of itself is a wonderful opportunity for you to complain for two. You will offer your spouse and their family so many insights into a long and rich culture that values meats both pickled and smoked.

The merging of families and religions is serious business, of course. But through millennia, it has been the gentile who has both challenged what we are willing to do on a Saturday and satisfied the need to disappoint our mothers. Many Nice Jewish Boys and Girls still feel trepidation about marrying outside the religion, but let me tell you, once you go goy, you'll jump for joy.

The Joys of Marrying
OUTSIDE THE TRIBE

by NOAH SEGAN,
actor and director

Workin' the Schmatta Biz

"To make it big in fashion as a Jew, convince the world you're a Protestant."

YOU CAN'T GO TO THE track without wearing clothes. It's an unfortunate truth, but a truth nonetheless. Even worse, textiles are kryptonite for Old Jewish Men. They can't see thread without trying to rebrand it and resell it at a markup. Take any blank fabric, stained or not, and an OJM will sew a little horsey or a black dog into it and tell you some incredible fakakta story about the shirt being extremely rare, "hand-stitched," and once owned by Jon Voight. This is a rich tradition, and it's your job to know how to buy a pack of crappy Kirkland undershirts from Costco and resell 'em as "high fashion" for a tenfold profit on the street. Remember, stories were made to be exaggerated.

Think Yiddish, Dress British

Ralph Lauren showed all the WASPs how to dress like a mensch, and he's one of only a handful of Jews knighted by the Queen of England. Only in America can a poor yid who grew up keeping Shabbos and kosher, schooled in Talmud with little exposure to high society, become the

prematurely gray fella steering generations of blue bloods toward the Jewish version of prep. It's always the short guys, isn't it?

If you ever thought Ralph Lauren was a European label, you're not alone. Ralph somehow convinced the movers and shakers all over the world that his brand is British-sophisticated. Now that's a Yiddish coup! According to Ralph, "People ask how a Jewish kid from the Bronx can do preppy clothes. Does it have to do with class and money? It has to do with dreams." But mostly a firm handshake.

From Lifshitz to Lauren

Dumping "Lifshitz" was probably Ralph's first smart move in a lifetime of excellent business decisions. These days, there's less risk in holding onto that Yiddishe name—unless of course you work in fashion, because no one's spending $200 on a set of bedroom slippers with *Murmelstein* stitched on the toe. What about perfume? What do you think smells better: Chanel, or Blumpkinsky? It's hard to upsell a product that sounds like a skin infection. Say what you want about Old Jewish Men who changed their names, but if Lauren had stayed Lifshitz, there is no doubt that we wouldn't have the greatest Jewish clothing brand in the world, and he most definitely wouldn't have a section in this "book."

Here's the honest truth: No matter how hard you try, you're never gonna be Ralph Lifshitz or Calvin Klein. Doesn't matter how smart you think you are, or how fantastic of a dresser people say you are, or how many grieving widows you seduced at Seymour Lunkman's funeral—it's not gonna happen. Why? The worst thing that ever happened to entrepreneurs is the seed round. These kids today don't know how to brawl. Forget investors. Learn to sweat. Go broke. Build it yourself.

QUIZ: WHAT KIND OF SCHMATTA DIGNITARY ARE YOU?

☐ Loafers   ☑ Sneakers

☑ Denim jacket   ☐ Blazer

☑ White hair   ☐ Dye job

☐ Private plane   ☑ Antique sports car collection

C O N G R A T U L A T I O N S !
You were born in a lower-middle-class neighborhood in New York City and now own the biggest clothing company in the world.

NO NEGOTIATING with *Larry*

by MEL OTTENBERG,
editor in chief of *Interview* magazine

I ALWAYS WANTED LARRY DAVID on the cover of *Interview*. There could be no better cover and we all know this. But Larry said no. Twice. Two different years. Both brutal blows to my soul. It's amazing that I could get out of bed and keep going after those brutal rejections. Obviously I'm kidding but also not really. Anyways, that's why we love Larry—he don't give a shit and would never waste his time getting a glow-up like the cover of *Interview* magazine. I love you, Lar!

SWINGING IT OUT AT

The Jazz Club

"Bass solos have no place in society."
—Rabbi Joseph B. Soloveitchik, purportedly

I**T'S NOT A PROPER NIGHT** out without telling the club owner to turn the music down, calling the cover charge "outrageous," changing seats three times to avoid the air-conditioning, or sending back the cheese plate.

Whether you live in New York, have a layover in London, got stuck in a Chicago snowstorm, or waddled onto the Amtrak for a weekend trip to Montreal, you need to know how to sniff out good jazz. While you don't gotta be an expert on the facts—no one expects you to recall who played keys on "Red Clay" or what year Bill Evans kicked the can—you'd better have a strong opinon for every note played.

ANDRÉ PREVIN

BUDDY RICH

LEE KONITZ

STAN GETZ

AT THE VILLAGE VANGUARD

"Musicians used to wear suits, you know."

"If the Vanguard goes under, New York is done."

"Another drum solo? They trying to kill me?"

"For forty dollars you should be able to see the piano player's hands!"

"You know, the woman who owned this place recently passed. Ran the place herself. She was Jewish."

All in the Feel

Memorize a few hip names on the modern jazz scene like Bix Beiderbecke, Jelly Roll Morton, Earl Hines, Joe "King" Oliver, and Sidney Bechet. Learn the lingo in case you meet a tall, red-lipsticked seductress in the smoky glow of the Zinc Bar or Café Carlyle, and then sidle over to her table, light her cigarillo with a shaky hand, and invite her to "trade fours" back at your place. If she doesn't sock you in the nose, unload some hip jazz analysis like, "Boy, that kid on the horn is the cat's meow!" Remember, jazz is all in the feel.

If I Wanted Aerobics, I'd Go for a Swim

Aerobic jazz is the late-night junk you hear at so-called hip clubs around the world where they think playing fast is playing good. It's a bunch of fellas on stage blowing sax lines and pounding the keys without saying anything musical. If an OJM is gonna bother schlepping to a jazz club, there better be a real show, not some improvised jam session—especially if they paid big to get in the door. Never shell out twenty-five bucks for a quartet that's up there bullshitting through changes. Oh, you never met before? If you want an OJM to travel, how about a rehearsal?

Will Schlep for Ear Food

Outside of big cities, in places like the Hudson Valley, the Hamptons, or the Berkshires, you'll see OJM at outdoor venues like Tanglewood lounging in camping chairs, sipping cold wine, munching overpriced cheese, and complaining about people blocking their view of the stage. The Newport Jazz Festival is one of the few completely out-of-the-way places on Earth where you will find Old Jewish Men, even though they're sure to be hiding from the sun under tents, faces gobbed with sunscreen. These are the rare moments in life when OJM can almost enjoy themselves in the company of a large group, although they always have an exit plan and a sure way to beat traffic. There's something about the combination of the outdoors, bearable music, and a good spread that makes life worth living. At least for the next hour or so.

GREAT JAZZ CLUBS WITH DISGUSTING BATHROOMS

1. **ZINC BAR:** The urinals make Port Authority smell like Versailles.

2. **SMALLS:** Putrid, swampy floors and a poor flush. Oy.

3. **MEZZROW:** One toilet that's right next to the bar. Who's the architectural genius behind this disaster?

4. **BLUE NOTE:** You gotta climb some stairs? Ageist. Time for a remodel.

"If the place is too clean the music's gonna stink. Jazz clubs should smell like a foot. The crummier the better."

—*Manny "Yammy" Funkerman,* 89, longtime New York jazz fan

MISTER *Show Business*

by DAVE SCHILLING, journalist

SAMMY DAVIS JR. might not immediately pop into your brain when someone mentions the term "Old Jewish Man," but he certainly qualified. As a biracial Jewish man of a certain age, Sammy was one of the few celebrities I could fully identify with (Lenny Kravitz converted to Christianity, so let's just move on from that). Plus, he had style and swagger for days. Have I often considered the sartorial benefits of an eye patch? Yes, of course. Who among us hasn't?

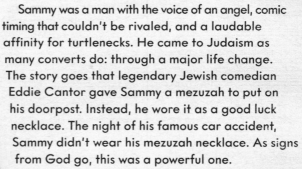

Sammy was a man with the voice of an angel, comic timing that couldn't be rivaled, and a laudable affinity for turtlenecks. He came to Judaism as many converts do: through a major life change. The story goes that legendary Jewish comedian Eddie Cantor gave Sammy a mezuzah to put on his doorpost. Instead, he wore it as a good luck necklace. The night of his famous car accident, Sammy didn't wear his mezuzah necklace. As signs from God go, this was a powerful one.

In 1960, Sammy converted and lived the remainder of his life as a landsman and son of Abraham. There's a photo of Sammy kissing the Western Wall that I really need to get framed for my home. It's inspiring, and not just because of Sammy's fame or wealth. It's because one of the reasons he became the greatest Old Black Jewish Man (OBJM) of them all is because he saw the commonalities between the two cultures he and I share. The struggles of Black people and the Jewish diaspora are well documented. They're major parts of not just American history, but world history in the broadest sense. At a time when public figures seek to divide our two peoples, it's more vital than ever to remember Sammy Davis Jr., who chose to be a part of a second oppressed minority. What a choice! To be miserable and to suffer willingly. Is there anything more Jewish than that?

Catchin' a Flick

SHARING FOND MEMORIES OF GOING to the pictures as a youngster, back when they actually made good movies, is an endless conversation piece. Films like *The Apartment* and *12 Angry Men* are still fresh in your mind, but movie theaters are too cold these days, the bathrooms are too far from the auditorium, they don't carry Swedish Fish, and the parking is worse than lousy.

If you're gonna schlep to a matinee, it's gotta be the right theater in the right neighborhood, on the right day at the right time, on a big screen with comfortable chairs, no people, fresh popcorn, and a coffee machine—so choose wisely. Stick to the joints that have been around awhile and forget the flashy megaplexes your grandkids tell you about. New movies are all junk. Nothing compares to catching a weekday matinee of *Gunfight at the O.K. Corral* in mid-October when the leaves are just right. *Das Boot* is a close second.

Top 5 Places to Pass Gas Without Anyone Hearing or Smelling

1 MOVIE THEATERS

2 DEPARTMENT STORES

3 SUBWAYS

4 AIRPLANES

5 COFFINS

FILM FORUM: THE LAST STAND

Here's one of the last OJM strongholds in Lower Manhattan. Catch a 12:15 matinee of *Midnight Cowboy* and join in the chorus of wet coughs, unapologetic seat adjustments, constant bathroom visits, pocket-rustling for homemade snacks and pills, and endless pointing at the screen, followed by the words, *Dustin Hoffman's Jewish! Is Ratso a real name or a nickname*? Bonus: You'll get helpful dialogue clarification throughout all screenings, complaints about previews, loud comments about recognizable donor names, and wild bickering—"SHHHH!!"—over a Pauline Kael review from 1971.

Turn It Up!

Before the movie starts, make sure to force your way into the projection booth so you can tell the kid running the reel to boost the volume all the way up. You gotta clearly hear every distinct round fired from Yul Brynner's pistol. Burt Lancaster's shotgun too.

It's a Theater, Not a Restaurant

New flicks are nauseating with all the computer graphics and fancy explosions, but worry not—Old Jewish Men don't watch that crap unless they financed it. These days, all the new pictures are like being on a roller coaster or inside a pinball machine, and to make the moviegoing experience even worse, they serve dinner too! The dinner meal is meant to be eaten in restaurants or at home, not in movie theaters. If, however, you break down from hunger in the third act and need to order a burrito, there's no need to fret: Cinema stereo systems are loud and sophisticated enough to cover up the sound of you passing gas. If someone complains about the horrible stench, blame it on the guy eating the turkey potpie in row 4.

MUSEUMS
THE NATURAL SEDATIVE

No one knows exactly why or how Old Jewish Men end up at museums all around the world, but there they are, futzing around the Ancient Egypt wing. At this very moment, some fella's picking his nose in front of the *Mona Lisa*, slapping his face awake near *Guernica*, furrowing his brow at the plaque his brother-in-law donated, popping Dramamine and nervously riding the escalator at Le Centre Pompidou, or scratching his tuchus at the Tate Modern. Luckily, there's hope for you among the endless abstractions and tiny placards that everybody hurts their back leaning over to skim.

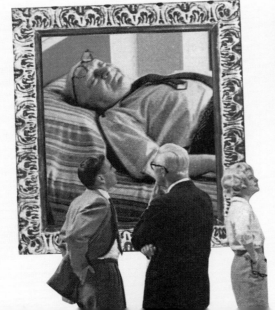

Guggenheim Starter Pack

Skip the Line

Visiting giant museums like the Met, the Louvre, or the Prado means you're not seeing a painting—you're seeing a line. There are lines for parking, lines for tickets, lines for the coat check, lines in front of a so-called masterpiece. Museums are nothing but congregations of annoying people competing for space, and it's your duty not to wait for anything. Yes, lines are for suckers, but fortunately you're not the average person. You're an Old Jewish Man, and if you really want to play up your ailments to the doctor, you might get the coveted MV-664.1 parking permit.

Right This Way, Sir

With the cynical and otherwise inappropriate use of the MV-664.1, not only can you park directly in front of the museum, but you can skip the entrance lines and waddle right up to *The Starry Night*. If some lowly ticket taker should question you, complain about your arthritic hip and then shout that there's "not enough handrails" and you almost fell over, which is discrimination! If that doesn't work, pretend like you're close friends with the president of the museum or say you donated the rifles in the American wing.

Bring a Sweater

Museums are frigid, sterile places with hard floors and not enough water fountains. When you're freezing to death in the oppressive air-conditioning or blowing your nose in the itchy dryness of Los Angeles's prized LACMA, go search for a place that isn't too hot or too cold. It's impossible. Or, at the very least, window-shop the pastry offerings at the museum coffee shop—anything to escape the mind-numbing maze of nap-inducing white walls. Fortunately, whoever dragged you to one of these places—whether it be the wife, self-important friends, or an annoying houseguest—will owe you one. And you can use this outing against them to prevail in an argument at a later date. This is how you win.

NEW YORK CITY ART MUSEUM TOILET RATINGS

1. **THE MET:** On the house (if you're a New Yorker)

2. **NEUE GALERIE:** Civilized

3. **AMERICAN MUSEUM OF NATURAL HISTORY:** Prehistoric (you get what you pay for)

4. **GUGGENHEIM:** Nauseating, even the golden toilet

5. **MOMA:** Monochromatic

6. **THE WHITNEY:** No-frills

DEAD LAST: THE NEW MUSEUM. A valiant effort. We can thank a retired venture capitalist for his six-figure gift to the museum that helped build the bathrooms, which were christened the Jerome L. and Ellen Stern Restrooms in his and his wife's name. Said Stern, "I'm eighty-three, and I thought it would be nice to see my name in a place where I'm going to spend a lot of time."

Grumpy Intellectuals

"At a certain point, you have to face the fact that you've turned into an old fart."

—ROBERT GOTTLIEB

CUE THE GERSHWIN, AHEM. *Chapter one. He adored being grumpy . . .* No pictures, no pictures. As a rule, don't approach these fellas for selfies at Barney Greengrass. But if you can't help yourself, prepare to be humiliated. *Get the hell away from me* is a mantra for these nearsighted, self-serious, highly irritable intellectuals with small friend groups, clanky typewriters, and daily routines that make the sixty-hour workweek look like a game of pickleball. You don't write and direct seventy movies, bang out dozens of novels, and compose operas, musicals, and symphonies as a backslapping, glad-handing partygoer with a Talmud-sized bill of divorce. You either stick to the same spouse, isolate in Connecticut, or pursue meaningless one-offs with young goyim who know the deal. That's right, productivity is a calculation, and it's how these fellas stay on top for so long.

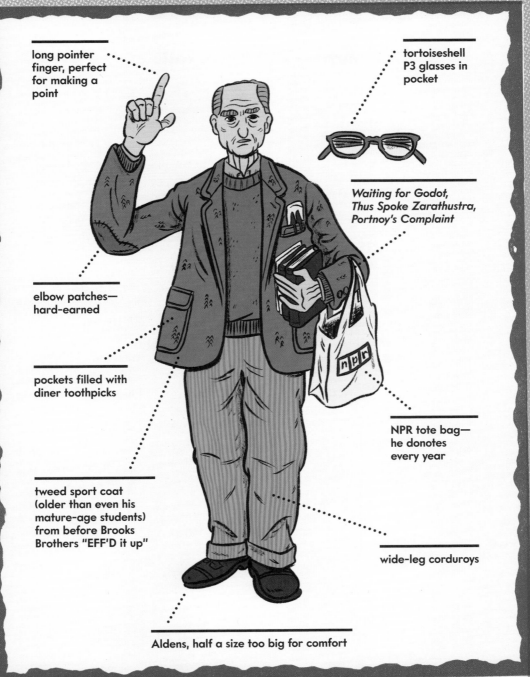

long pointer finger, perfect for making a point

tortoiseshell P3 glasses in pocket

Waiting for Godot, Thus Spoke Zarathustra, Portnoy's Complaint

elbow patches— hard-earned

pockets filled with diner toothpicks

NPR tote bag— he donotes every year

tweed sport coat (older than even his mature-age students) from before Brooks Brothers "EFF'D it up"

wide-leg corduroys

Aldens, half a size too big for comfort

Consistency Is Key

This crusty OJM variety thrives on predictable experiences at Elaine's, Film Forum, the New York Public Library, the Russian Tea Room, and Gracie's Corner Diner. Food stopped having taste thirty years ago so you can *forget* the specials. If it was so special, it'd be on the menu! (Right, Jerry?)

These fellas have lunch at the same time every day with the same faces—give or take a few mistresses over the years. No new friends. No new clothes. No new nothin'. Habit is a religion: soft-boiled eggs, melon, cottage cheese, drip coffee, still water without ice, corn muffin toasted with no butter. Reliable. Light. Non-fried. Work is life, life is work, and they need every day to be like yesterday. Their timeless moth-infested closets are lined with rows of big, clean slacks, tucked-in oxfords, smart shoes, and lived-under bucket caps, umbrellas, and big glasses. They mourned the loss of their anonymity decades ago, but still want it back.

OBIT by EMMANUEL IVANSTEIN, *New York Times*

MR. GRUMPY INTELLECTUAL DIES AS THE MOST FAMOUS JEWISH AMERICAN WRITER,

even though it is not known whether he ever did anything Jewish. His previous marriages——to the actress Cornelia Waspnose, the actress Sally Sailboat, the actress Phobia V. Christian, and the equestrian Sloane T. Sandwich——ended in divorce. He had no children, but the memory of every tiny detail of his life will be carried into the future by his entirely autobiographical novels.

Embrace Your
INNER PETTY KING

by SUZY WEISS, reporter, *The Free Press*

OBJECTING TO SPLITTING THE BILL EQUALLY when you didn't have anything to drink. Keeping a tally of the number of toilet paper rolls the love of your life has gone through this month (4.5 as of Thursday). Quibbling over whose turn it is to take the dog for a walk, even though you didn't do it last time or two times ago (it was raining). Is there any better use of time than keeping a lifelong tab of every day-to-day grievance? Surely. But while some may call it a waste, fixating on each and every wrong is more than the principle—it's an art.

Being rather, how should I say this, *sensitive* to life's little details, like winning a Nobel Prize or always knowing the location of the nearest exit, certainly isn't a result of being Jewish, but it isn't unrelated either. Still, no one should be ashamed of being petty. Embrace it. Contrary to popular opinion, it's a different category altogether than being cheap, a nag, ungenerous, a worrywart, or a stickler. It's more that when someone says they're running ten minutes late but they show up eighteen minutes later holding a coffee from the café down the street . . . well, that information is merely noticed, weighed, and deposited into one or another balancing pan on the scales of justice that live in your mind and are updating constantly. If, that is, you're petty.

The key is to choose your battles wisely and make sure they're small ones. Insignificant, almost. Get granular. Ask to see the terms of service. It doesn't matter that it cost eleven dollars and that there's a thirty-day return policy—you're simply not going home without a refund. That way, when it comes to the real big-ticket items, with the reputation you'll have earned, you won't even have to bother checking the bill.

"Whatever gratification that comes with being a religious leader can't possibly be worth the cost."

—*Boris Mandelbaum*, 102, Bialystoker shul regular, vested into an annual membership rate of thirty-two cents

CHAPTER 2

King of the Temple

Maybe you got aspirations to be a shul-going big shot. Prez? Board member? Spiritual guru? The guy holding the Torah? Kiddush sponsor? Not every fella wants to rule the shul, but all Old Jewish Men want recognition when they get called up for an aliyah, or, at the very least, someone to chat with during kiddush. So make sure that tefillin's kosher and your tallis is pressed.

Get a mug and stick with it. No one touches your mug.

side yarmulke

Massive hairy forearms

Read the paper that agrees with all of your opinions.

Heavy Lies the Crown

If you're looking to become the true king of the shtiebel, know that it comes at a price: You gotta schlep to shul every Friday night and Saturday morning to make minyan-shuckling numbers, make yourself reasonably available for board meetings, schmooze and make moves to raise funds, and kiss the heads of newly cut babies. Respect doesn't come cheap.

But don't confuse a temple Big Shot with an Undercover Macher or a Beloved Old-Timer with a Schnorrer. There are key distinctions between these types, so you better figure out pretty quickly which one you are. As the Torah says: "Master thy stereotype and thou shall prosper, and so on, et cetera."

Big Shots

"Make sure I get the leftovers"

Undercover Machers

FIG. 2

34

OJM TEMPLE TALK

If you haven't been to shul since your bar mitzvah almost sixty years ago, here's a refresher course. Call it Synagogue Speak 101, so cut the line and elbow your way to the spread. (Who sponsored it again?)

Bema: the altar

Bris: circumcision

Cholent: a meaty slop served on Shabbos

Davening: reciting of prayers (these should be mumbled incoherently)

Kibbitz: to chat

Mechitzah: the barrier that separates men and women at synagogue (you're there to pray, not leer)

Minchah: afternoon prayers

Mitzvah: a good deed (do this once a month or so, no need to go overboard)

Shacharit: morning prayers, no one's done it since Moses

Shtiebel: a smaller, less formal synagogue

Shuckle: to sway during Jewish prayer (use those hips)

Shul: Yiddish for synagogue (please tell me you know that one)

Skach: sukkah covering

Spread: the size and quality of the food being served; the thing everyone complains about later

Sukkah: a temporary shelter covered in natural materials, built near a synagogue or house; used especially for meals during the Jewish festival of Sukkoth (aka "hut week")

The BIG SHOT

"I DONATED THAT"

SHUL PROFILE: *Shacharit*? Never heard of her. Hasn't opened a prayer book since his bar mitzvah. Circulates seats during the service to network and hunt for new clients. Averages four (4) bathroom visits per hour. Phone in pocket, only takes it out in the can.

TYPICAL JOB: Real estate wheeler/dealer, jewelry business, entertainment lawyer, Hollywood agent, restaurateur, textiles (carpets or garments), media personality

MOTTO: "How long does this usually go?"

SINGS OR HUMS?: Sings

HAIRSTYLE: White, brushed back, and feathered

SNACK OF CHOICE: Anything with a crunch

This Torah was generously and anonymously donated by Ari Weissenbaum and Family on the occasion of his daughter's bat mitzvah that took place at the Beverly Hills Hotel and alcohol was $200 a head.

Plaque idea to make you seem humble.

Making an Entrance

OJM Big Shots tend to be on the larger side: big-armed, wide-shouldered, and plump-wristed. They wear fancy European watches and waddle like a thick-thighed duck. A true Big Shot doesn't show up on time and will usually appear right before the Torah reading or even in the middle. The entrance should interrupt the service for at least 1–3 minutes as they shake hands with absolutely everybody—doesn't matter if they've met them one hundred times or never at all, they gotta treat everyone like a lifelong best friend. Even if they forget a person's name, Big Shots are known for summoning tiny, strange details to convince people they care: *Your mother's from Cincinnati, they have a nice bridge there, don't they? Did you end up winning that canasta tournament? Still living in Delray?*

Making an Exit

As a Big Shot, you should never be seen singing "Lecha Dodi" at the end of services. Why? Because you know to pack up your tallit bag right after kaddish and scamper downstairs to plant that flag next to the spread. Anyone who has ever been to synagogue knows the thing Jews most consistently and unfailingly give a crap about is the spread. And at most shuls, the heart of the kiddush spread is the table with the lox, bagels, and condiments. Forget doggie bags—bring a tractor trailer. Thanks for sponsoring, Ira and Karen Bernstein!

If you're a gentile reading this book—next time buy two copies—you're probably confused as to why the hordes aren't crammed around the beverage table, fighting over the Tanqueray bottle. Well, most Jews typically aren't big drinkers, unless of course it's an open bar. (Drinks are where they get ya!) They're salt and carbohydrate people. Sure, they make a *l'chaim* or two on Shabbos, but no one's getting plastered. Jews eat. Gentiles booze.

Delivering the Speech

If the Big Shot is shelling out for kiddush, they wanna talk. These guys love to hear themselves yak. Their speech may go a little something like this: "I'll keep this short and sweet, just like my wife, minus the sweet. Hold the applause. Thank you, thank you. Little more applause, actually. Anyway, what a wonderful community we have here. When I was growing up, we never had enough, but you can get used to anything. Well, almost anything—New York without air-conditioning is tough. At my age I only want the best for myself and those I love, that's why I like to sponsor kiddush whenever I can. It's nothing for me. So enjoy this terrific spread. As you can see, I didn't skimp: thirteen different kinds of herring, some beautiful nova lox, four different kinds of schmear. Eight different kinds of bagels. Poppy seed, garlic, egg, we got it all. Onion. The works. This is what life's all about. Being together. Eating good food that I spent a trunkful of cash on. L'chaim and good Shabbos."

Kiddush Spreads Around the World

AUSTRALIA: Industrial pot cholent, kishkes, assortment of herring, cakes, crackers, soda, seltzer

ISRAEL: Cream herring, mustard herring, white wine herring, Israeli salad, cheese and crackers, mango juice, apple juice, seltzer, Coke Zero, lox

UK: Fish balls, potato kugel, sweet kugel, cholent, herring, lox, bagels

FRANCE: Couscous with apricots and other pretentious crap

UNDERCOVER MACHER
The ANONYMOUS DONOR

SHUL PROFILE: Shacharit over Mincha, sits near the middle on the aisle, averages one (1) bathroom trip per hour, goes with the hordes to kiddush, last to eat, a real mensch

TYPICAL JOB: High-level businessman, mathematician, economist, financier, scientist, logician

MOTTO: "Money screams, wealth whispers"

TUCKED/UNTUCKED: Tucked

HAIRSTYLE: The Bloomberg

SNACK OF CHOICE: Lightly salted almonds/cashews

Making an Entrance

Being an Undercover Macher is trickier and a lot less fun than being a Big Shot, but it comes with a different kind of respect and recognition. You gotta be patient.

These fellas like to be on time, savoring the brisk, solitary walk to synagogue. They are small of stature and svelte, as they take care of themselves, don't overeat, and participate in light exercise. They like to be one of the first ten men to arrive at shul and love to make the minyan. If they suspect there won't be a minyan, Undercover Machers will call friends the night before to ask if they can make it. If that doesn't work, they'll phone their local casting agent for some semitic-looking stand-ins. Whatever works.

Making an Exit

They may be punctual, but you're dead wrong if you think an Undercover Macher hangs around until the service is over. These gents have got things to do on Shabbos, like golf, catch late-afternoon baseball games, and read the *Journal*. So if you plan on ducking out of shul early, do as they do: Quietly pack your tallit bags and exit before the Torah reading. If someone tries to shake your hand on the way out—which will happen—do *one single pump* with vigor and silent, direct eye contact. NOTE: No matter whose hand you're shaking, sanitize immediately with the tiny bottle of Purell you carry everywhere.

Poking Around the Sable

Unlike Big Shots, Undercover Machers will rarely stick around for kiddush. On the rare occasion that you do see one of these fellas nosing around the spread, you may notice that he won't take heaping helpings of lox, cream cheese, cookies, cakes, kugel, whitefish, and egg salad. An Undercover Macher eats like a bird. He pokes at his food, deconstructing sandwiches and never finishing entire bagels. He thinks carefully and analytically about everything, including the nosh.

Running the Shul

Undercover Machers have final say over choosing the budget, the rabbi, and their salary. This is why they *cannot* understand why Big Shots continually interrupt the shul service with their incessant, obnoxious chatter. In fact, the two types are always butting heads during synagogue meetings. As an Undercover Macher, you think of the rabbi as an employee, while a Big Shot wants to be friends with everyone. But guess what? Transaction makes the world go round.

Look, the rabbi is a guy with a job to do: inspire the congregation and be charming enough to get them in the door. If he fails at this simple task, you cut the cord. The value of a shul begins and ends with the fella on the bema—that's showbiz, kid.

The BELOVED OLD-TIMER
ANOTHER OJM CLASSIC

EVERY SHUL HAS AT LEAST ONE. NO ONE KNOWS MUCH ABOUT this fella; he always projects an air of mystery. If you're a Beloved Old-Timer, people will speculate about you, so play it up a bit. Since you could be anywhere between the age of seventy-seven and one hundred and you spend your twilight years doing G-d knows what, mess with people when they ask you what you did over the week. Say you "got some last night," but don't specify what you got. Tell them you worked in the defense industry, but don't say in which country. Make it all up on the spot—people assume that geriatrics are honest. It's your job to jumble fact and fiction. No one can nail you down, so have fun with it.

TUCKED/UNTUCKED: Accidental half-tuck

MOTTO: "You're young and then you're old and then you're young again"

LIFE FORCE: Talkin' turkey with the youngsters, snoring loudly, and being nudged awake when called up to the Torah

FOR KICKS: Bobbles the Torah every once in a while during hagbah to keep the congregation on their toes

CHARITY: AT THE END OF THE DAY, IT'S A TAX WRITE-OFF

Whichever Old Jewish Man you're aching to be, there's something you gotta know: It doesn't matter how much bread you got. OJM give back no matter what. It's not a lump sum, it's a percentage of what you have, and if you think you're getting away with something by not giving dough to charity, well . . . that's on you, fella. And no, you can't adjust charity for inflation!

The OJM Apprenticeship Program encourages all its members to give away at least 10 percent of their money (11 percent if you're a real macher). But there's good news: It's a write-off! And, who knows, if all this heaven and G-d stuff is real, you're setting yourself up for a prettyyyyy nice spot up there. Don't be a schmuck—give. Or, be a schmuck, but still give to charity.

ABC: Always Be Confusing

As a Beloved Old-Timer, you may or may not have any idea what the hell's going on at any given time. So drop little bits of bullshit wisdom along the way, leaving a trail of nonsense like mouse excrement. You can always count on a Beloved Old-Timer to say baffling things to young people, such as "Life is over—then it ends," and then walk away. Cryptic.

These fellas embraced their inner jokester years ago, knowing full well that messing with people will extend their lives. If you think cute old men don't work on being adorable, you're living in a fantasy world. A master Beloved Old-Timer understands how to appear oblivious and innocent, especially to the beautiful younger ladies at shul.

The Art of Mumbling Kinda Creepy Things

Mumbling stuff under your breath is a craft—try not to make it too obvious. And if you're gonna leer, you better be wearing thick eyeglasses or have a little bit of a hunch. Here are a couple of "Did he just say that?!" standbys:

- "Did you get a whiff of her breath? Smells like schmaltz herring. Incredible."

- "I've never seen such a beautiful woman scarf down liver like that."

- "Oh to be fifty-five again . . ."

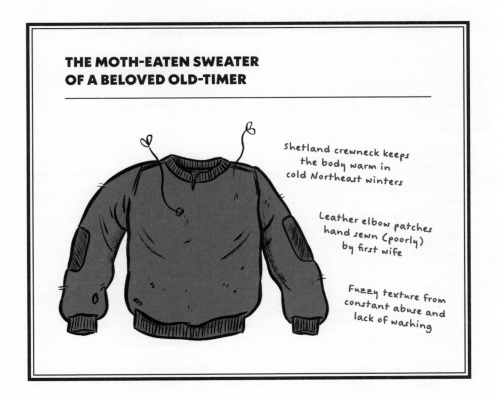

THE MOTH-EATEN SWEATER OF A BELOVED OLD-TIMER

shetland crewneck keeps the body warm in cold Northeast winters

Leather elbow patches hand sewn (poorly) by first wife

Fuzzy texture from constant abuse and lack of washing

The SCHNORRER

EVERY SHUL'S GOT ONE

TUCKED/UNTUCKED: Untucked all the time

KIDDISH FOODS EVERY SCHNORRER KNOWS TO SLIDE INTO THEIR SUIT COAT POCKET: Hand-torn challah chunks, black and white cookies, bagels, assorted fruits

MOTTO: "Are you sure you don't want it? If you don't want it, I'll take it."

LIFE FORCE: Herring in white sauce, herring in cream sauce, beelining for the can when the bill comes

You Gonna Eat That?

Flip on that motormouth and don't turn it off. Every congregation has at least five of these eighty-something-year-old fellas zooming around the kiddush table, pushing their way to the lox spread. The Schnorrer may be easily mistaken for any number of other badly dressed men at shul, so pinning this particular species down can be difficult. Luckily, some key personality traits and accessories are dead giveaways.

A true Schnorrer truly appreciates Jewish community in a way that few can understand, and they will rarely crack off-color jokes. But this doesn't mean a Schnorrer can't say otherwise disgusting things, which to them is just called "making conversation." Detailed rundowns of bodily mishaps, miscues, or colonoscopy prep are run-of-the-mill. Buckle up!

That Mysterious Schnorrer Charm

Life hasn't been easy for these fellas, and unlike Undercover Machers and Big Shots, they live on hope, chance, and the generosity of others. Being a Schnorrer means having an arsenal of surprising stories of varying tone. These anecdotes are often disgusting but also wise and heartfelt. A Schnorrer should leave conversations abruptly, before the story comes to a natural end. This will leave others feeling puzzled, perhaps even with the faint desire to speak to the Schnorrer again. It's all part of the charm.

Shabbos Best

As far as wardrobe, an authentic shul Schnorrer takes great pride in wearing his standard-issue Shabbos uniform on Friday night and Saturday morning: a tattered shirt, broken-down shoes, soggy untied shoelaces, tape-repaired glasses, and a hat from the Ottoman Empire. Despite this failed attempt at style, a Schnorrer isn't fooling anyone. After all, a Schnorrer doesn't know he's a Schnorrer, which is key.

Life Is Kinda Worth Living

Unlike other types of fellas you're sure to meet at shul, Schnorrers fall ass-backward into their Schnorrer-dom. Schnorrers simply wake up one day as Schnorrers, and it takes them half a lifetime, if ever, to recognize what they have become. Some say that being oblivious to one's own condition is a survival tactic, but who knows. Bask in whatever fate chooses. Keep shoving that leftover kiddush herring into your suit pants pockets.

Other Notables

The Seat Snatcher

Go buy a good alarm clock. These fellas have one concern at shul: getting a prime seat. A top-notch location (up front, to the left of the bimah, not in direct eyeline of the rabbi) means you're part of the action. Seat Snatchers see synagogue as a show rather than a ceremony: the rabbi is the lead guitar, the cantor is the soloist, and an aliyah is a sing-along. For these fellas, the experience is the seat and the seat is the experience. Without the right seat they have failed, and with it they have succeeded. Live and die by the seat.

Get ready to fast for 40 days when clumsy Morty Golinkin drops the Torah.

The Torah Guy

Here's another adored member of the congregation. More often than not, the Torah Guy is a Holocaust survivor, and he *loves* the Torah. Not, say, the Five Books of Moses, or whatever the parsha is that week—he loves the physical Torah itself. Yep, he donated that one up on the bimah. And isn't she a beauty? Crimson-velvet covering and the two bronze hats that go on top—that costs extra, you know? Who's first up for hagbah?

The Other Torah Guy

This fella keeps up with the parsha and loves his biblical heroes. The cutest thing about him is how much he believes. It's not a cynical or intellectual belief either; he's earnest in his genuine love of the Torah and all its teachings. He brings printed articles and will want to talk to the rabbi about his sermon. You'll find him bent over the Tanach with coffee after kiddush, banging hard on the table during benching. He's a sweetheart. He's also single. Very single. Know anybody?

The Sukkah Overseer

Directly after Yom Kippur break-fast, this fella transforms with the flick of a lulav from a repenting Jew into a sukkah general contractor. To pull off this incredible metamorphosis, the Sukkah Overseer tells people that he once worked as an engineer or managed teams of people, when the truth is he has never built or overseen the building of anything ever in his life. He walks around the break-fast table grilling people on their schedules for the upcoming week, telling them that "sukkah takes precedence over other obligations." When the day comes to erect the thing, the Sukkah Overseer is there early in the morning to boss people around, and once it's constructed he loves to eat and sleep in his sukkah, especially in the rain. Next year, let's get an earlier start, people!

The Bris Spread

Usually, a bris takes place early in the morning. You gotta get the foreskin chopped before everyone goes to work, which isn't a comfortable time to be at shul for most people. So to make it worth the indecent hour, the bris spread should be the best that money can buy. It's an unwritten rule that the parents shell out big bucks to appease the attendees who showed up to watch an infant get his foreskin lopped at the crack of dawn on a Tuesday. As an Old Jewish Man, it's your responsibility to hold the family accountable if the spread isn't up to snuff. Great-lookin' kid, by the way!

Tough Guys aka The Muscle

Tough Guys are the flat-nosed short kings with meat-cleaver hands and James Caan shoulder-hair bravado who take meetings in the shvitz. These fellas came of age on creaky floors in cramped Lower East Side tenements elbow to elbow with bird-boned Yiddish-speaking grandmothers but somehow made it to Harvard at age fifteen on a backgammon scholarship.

> ## "We're bigger than U. S. Steel."
>
> **—HYMAN ROTH**

They spent their early days on Grand Street bent over the Talmud in dingy synagogue basements with harsh lighting. They saw Judaism as a brotherhood where loyalty—not God—is king. In deep Brooklyn, Jewish gangsters like the Shapiro brothers carved their own version of the commandments on the walls of Brownsville and understood that the only way to make it in a world that moves against you is to rise and kill first.

This breed is always glaring and conspiring, especially while they eat. They live to eat, and there better be a dessert menu. And coffee with thick cream. They can't get enough of the stuff.

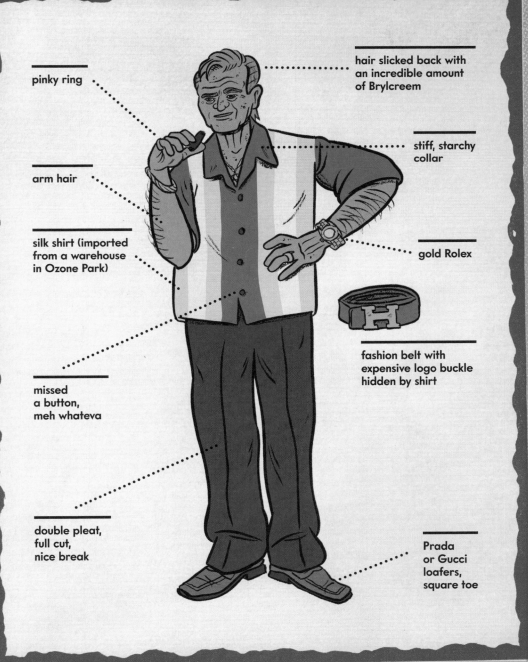

pinky ring

arm hair

silk shirt (imported from a warehouse in Ozone Park)

missed a button, meh whateva

double pleat, full cut, nice break

hair slicked back with an incredible amount of Brylcreem

stiff, starchy collar

gold Rolex

fashion belt with expensive logo buckle hidden by shirt

Prada or Gucci loafers, square toe

Tough Jews Love Meatballs

At diners and luncheonettes, Tough Guys sit in the back so they can see the action. They stuff arteries just like Romans—everything rinsed in sauce and covered in salt. Heavy cream suntans morning coffee beside a plate of fried eggs bathed in grease. In the turn-of-the-century days, Tough Guys and Italians were practically indistinguishable, like Chico and Harpo. Back then, they had a criminal brotherhood and did favors for each other. But while Italians in fine suits gathered in their mothers' restaurants, Jews congregated in the backs of smoky Brooklyn luncheonettes to plan the next grift. That or just chatting about their last trip to West Boca.

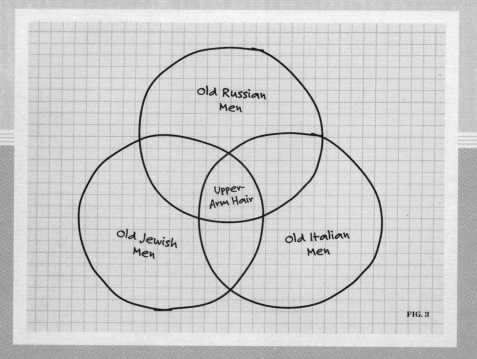

Old Russian Men

Upper Arm Hair

Old Jewish Men

Old Italian Men

FIG. 3

The Art of WEARING A *Chai*

by JASON DIAMOND, writer

HERE'S THE THING about wearing a Chai necklace: If you're going to wear one, then you need chest hair. This is in the Talmud. Well, not the Talmud itself, but in the "extras" section when you buy a copy of the deluxe Mishnah. It's in the part where the rabbis debate how to properly milk a goat. A Star of David you can do without the chest hair. But if you want to wear a Chai and it doesn't have a nice rug to settle in, then figure something out. There has to be a treatment you can do to grow chest hair. Perhaps consider chest hair plugs? That might be an option.

Either way, the Chai is a truly badass necklace and the one person who has ever been able to get away with having a totally bare chest when he wears one is Jon Bernthal in *The Wolf of Wall Street* because he's ripped and has some incredibly inspiring facial hair. If you're Jon Bernthal, then it's fine. Otherwise, consider rubbing some minoxidil between your man boobs.

OBIT by LENNY STEINWALD, *Atlantic City Weekly*

BY THE TWENTY-FIRST CENTURY,

Mr. Tough Guy's hairpiece had rusted to the yellow hue of a cheesecake. He remained at the battle station of his youth: a barstool on the second floor of the old Atlantic City casino Sutzkever's. Bernie, his favorite bartender, had died; Mr. Tough Guy's cronies, who once crowded around him cracking wise, had died; the gentile rivals they had plotted against also had died; Sutzkever's, in fact, had shuttered, the entire block where it was located had been condemned by the city, and the city, of course, had been forgotten.

Mr. Tough Guy didn't notice. He had perfected a streetwise, slanted glare, the art of saying nothing to nobody, and how to spit menacingly on the ground beside him. He had the run of the place——whether or not anybody remembered what the place was called.

CHAPTER 3

The OJM Deli Association ... and More

The deli is more than a joint you go to get a decent meal. It is a sanctuary, a vigor-restoring oasis for Old Jewish Men to sit for hours and be pampered with complimentary pickles, coleslaw, bottomless coffee, and all the sliced-up nitrates fit for a king. Your wife thinks you eat a dangerous amount of chopped liver and wants you to give it up—all the more reason to go. Remember: OJM don't cheat on their spouses with younger women, they cheat with Barney Greengrass.

This essential chapter is all about eating out. We'll look at deli dos and don'ts, the finer points of sitting in coffee shops, the cultural power center of OJM life that is the Chinese restaurant, and so much more.

This Place Has Terrible Service!

It's your job to be as irritable as possible with rookie waiters. Use any excuse to attack their character so that they get the message: *Never screw up an Old Jewish Man's order*. A waiter should have your table and sandwich ready to go when you walk in the door. That's the deal, and if they talk back, make a fuss. If they say you're being rude, double down and insult their haircut. It's disrespectful to ask an OJM if he's "*sure* he wants belly lox, not nova."* Questions like that deserve an unhinged rant, just like everything else.

Get Rid of the Youngsters

Making a hopeful young customer's deli experience as unpleasant as possible guarantees that they won't come back. Tourists? Talk about a field day. Nothing makes an Old Jewish Man happier than haranguing some Midwesterner for not knowing the difference between pastrami and corned beef, or for asking for lettuce and tomato on a Reuben. Go back to Des Moines, kid!

"I like young people, just not up close."

—The Greater OJM Community

The Platonic Ideal

A nearly dying deli that's been hanging on by a thread for over half a century is the ideal eatery for most Old Jewish Men. Requirements include plentiful seating, a menu that never changes, and low volume (except the sound of your own voice). Shuffle into a deli in New York, L.A., Chicago, or Montreal and you can quickly tell if it has the makings of a regular haunt. It doesn't take a genius to separate

* Nova (smoked) is for kids. Belly lox (cured in salt) is for men with knuckle hair.

the neighborhood standbys from the interlopers.

These days, the clientele has more to do with the way the neighborhood has changed rather than the restaurant itself. For example, the Upper West Side remains old and Jewish while the Lower East Side has become young and touristy—way too many morons running around clogging lines and smashing their burgers. Gramercy might have the most bagel stores per block in the city, but is it a good place to sit and argue? Don't count on it. The Upper West Side reigns supreme.

The Commute: There Isn't One

Don't leave the neighborhood unless you have to. You've known the local butcher, Izzy Pasternak, for years, and he doesn't put his thumb on the scale for your order like he does with all the new faces. Even if the new supermarket down the block's got the best deal in town, always go to your local. Loyalty counts for something, even when it hurts in the pocket.

Bitter Rivals

Your raison d'être, if you will, is to be recognized by the owners of your favorite establishments. So whether you reside on the Upper West Side, Côte Saint-Luc, North London, Pico-Robertson, or any other OJM hot spot, be careful where you frequent. To stay chummy with the deli brass, you can't let them know you visit their competitors. There's nothing better than glad-handing and chitchatting with the owners every time you walk in—not to mention the extra rugelach they give you on Hanukkah—so never let them see you wearing another team's colors. Pick a place to buy the essentials, and if you want something from somewhere else, send the Catholic kid in the apartment next door to get it for you. Just be careful out there. Everyone talks.

THE INVENTION OF SOUP

An OJM Fable

ARCHAEOLOGICAL evidence shows that soup was invented around 20,000 BCE in a cave somewhere in the Jiangxi province in China. The OJM Community, however, maintains a different theory: Soup was instead created in 1882 by a fella named Lenny Soupman of Brownsville, Brooklyn, with his wife, Rachel, and their twenty-seven kids.

It all started one evening when Lenny came home dead tired from a day of selling used toothpicks on Pitkin Avenue, whining of a sore throat. Rachel, busy washing and peeling hundreds of pounds of potatoes for their more than two dozen offspring, told her husband that she wouldn't be available for a few minutes to boil the water. Furious, Lenny shouted through his sore throat, "'A few minutes' is a few minutes too long!"

Chomping on a raw onion for sustenance (and sinus relief), Lenny spent the next several moments chewing and picking his nose, debating whether he should try to figure out how to heat up the water. Researchers claim that Lenny then began futzing around with the pot on the stove, pushing it pointlessly from one burner to the other, desperate to make something happen.

As Lenny stared mindlessly at the pot, something miraculous happened: A chunk of onion fell from his mouth and into the boiling water. The rest, as they say, is history.

Send It Back!

Your deli soup bowl better be piping hot and packed with flavor. Soup is for the soul, but it's also for the throat, and much like the fabled Lenny Soupman's frayed vocal cords, yours are sore from shouting at everyone. As you settle into OJM Soup Mode, remember that you have every right to send food back. And you can bet your bottom dollar that if the waitress skimmed from the top of the pot, it'll be making a U-turn back to the kitchen. Everyone knows that the meat bouillon settles at the bottom. After all, alte kakers are responsible for 99.9 percent of rejected food worldwide.

If the soup arrives medium-warm, send it back. If you can't taste the chicken fat, send it back. If the matzo balls are too dry, there's not enough onions, and they didn't give you saltines on the side, send it back. If everything else is okay, slurp away.

Kasha: The Great Groat Value Meal

Whoever said there's no food that's cheap, nutritious, *and* palatable wasn't a kasha eater. Buckwheat is the Russian starch of a cold winter, like the woman who won't leave you for a taller man. Reliable, sturdy, and unlikely to give you a heart attack on the spot. Sure, kasha lacks the beauty of jasmine rice or the elegance of a long spaghetti noodle, but it will stabilize your blood sugar and won't leave you in the dust. While most people are 70 percent water, Old Jewish Men are 70 percent kasha.

ARBITRARY SOUP RANKINGS BY IMPORTANCE

1

CHICKEN SOUP
with
MATZO BALLS
or KREPLACH

2

LENTIL

3

BORSCHT

4

KUBBEH

5

POTATO LEEK

Gary Gondlestein's No-Frills Classic Kasha

INGREDIENTS

- 1 cup toasted buckwheat groats
- 1¾ cups filtered water
- 1–2 tablespoons salted butter
- 30 pounds salt

DIRECTIONS

1. Mash it all together. Use your hand if you don't have a spoon.
2. Eat fast and without joy.

THE 4 BEST SOPPING VEHICLES AT THE DELI

Whether you're sopping up egg yolk or gravy or scraping out those last drops of soup, these are the breads you should be asking for at the deli:

1. Challah—heavy yet versatile

2. Rye—the old standby rarely lets us down

3. English muffin—provides an air of sophistication

4. Pita—warmed, not toasted

NOTE: Never sop with sourdough, seeded, or multigrain breads. Bagels are not good sopping agents.

That Sandwich Is Named After Me!

The greatest achievement in your life will be having a sandwich named in your honor. Forget real estate acquisitions, fatherhood, and sixtieth wedding anniversaries. Seeing your namesake up there on the deli menu means you put time in and are finally getting the respect you deserve. And the very best thing about having a delicious sandwich in your name is that your friends don't. Every time you eat with them, it's your duty to remind them of this highest distinction. It's a win-win, for you.

"Instead of getting a sandwich named after me, I opened a sandwich store. Sure, a sandwich is great, but the greatest honor for me as a Brooklyn Jew is to have a bagel shop. If you're not some bum and have a little chutzpah I might name a sandwich after you too. Just gotta ask. I'll probably say no, but it doesn't hurt to ask. That's the power of having your own shop, you can say no."

—*Julian Cavin-Zeidenstein*, owner of Greenberg's Bagels, on sandwich naming

Decent meat-to-bread ratio.

Welcome to the

DELI

ASSOCIATION

(NEW YORK DIVISION)

NOW THAT YOU'VE PASSED DELI 101, LET'S TAKE A closer look at some of the top-rated establishments approved by the Old Jewish Men's Deli Association of New York City (OJMDA-NYC Local 157). This is a society of nitrate-laden fellas who convene in dingy basements to argue about the state of the modern deli. The meetings are top secret, but outsiders speculate that they focus mostly on the price of lox, the dry babka epidemic, and the sudden drop in complimentary restaurant table pickles and coleslaw. (Sleep with one eye open, Saul Zabar.)

So, without further ado, here's a list of New York–based OJMDA-approved restaurants for your appetizing and noshing pleasure.

Russ & Daughters Appetizing

FOUNDED: 1914 by Joel Russ

WEEKLY SALES STATS:
Ten thousand truckloads of herring in mustard and dill, a cargo ship of black and whites, a Mack truck of bagels, and the occasional bagel chip

PRICE OF BELLY LOX BY THE POUND: Depends who's askin', pal!

TOP DOGS: Niki Russ Federman and Josh Russ Tupper, but Mr. Russ may still slice a pound or two

UNOFFICIAL MOTTO: "Always be opening more stores"

TOILET: Only at the new locations; there's no accessible can at the original Houston Street spot

Appetizing, Not Deli

This is the only place on earth owned by people who claim to know the difference between a deli and an appetizing store. If you wanna get thrown out of Russ & Daughters, order a pastrami on rye and see what happens. Doesn't matter if you've been going there for six months or six decades: Prepare to be heckled over the counter by Mr. Russ (he'll probably tell you to buy his book too). If you find yourself in a conversation with the family and wanna impress, tell them that a deli has something to do with meat, and an appetizing store has something to do with dairy . . . or something like that. Joel Russ himself didn't fully understand it.

What to Order, Who to Bribe

After muscling your way to the front of the line, it's your turn at the deli counter. Don't bother taking a number—that's for suckers who don't know what they want. Get right into the face of the counter jockey and scream your OJM Classic Order: *Half of a quarter of belly lox, plain cream cheese, and a salt bagel. Slice the bagel. Everything separate.*

While they're carving the lox, tell them to throw in a free pickle or two. If they say no, ask what they *can* add for free. If they say nothing, tell them you're never coming back. If they still don't care, threaten to sue and scream the word *harassment* a bunch of times.

Alternative order: buttered bialy with tuna fish.

JOSH RUSS TUPPER, RUSS & DAUGHTERS CO-OWNER, ON . . .

HOW TO SPOT A GENTILE: "You know them by their look of fear. These are the people who just waited in line for an hour and a half, and when they finally get their chance at the counter, they have no idea what they want. They freeze."

WHAT OLD JEWISH MEN SAY TO HIM ABOUT EXPANDING: "Don't do it. Why would you do that? You should open a store every hundred years."

OLD JEWISH MEN OF THE PAST: "They'd come in and say, 'Don't tell my wife I'm here.' Then they'd order a half pound of chopped liver, half pound of belly lox, choke it down, and be ill for a week."

The OJM Value Hack #3,201

If you're sitting at a café and want to enjoy yourself for hours without spending much, try this: Buy a fresh-out-of-the-oven bagel or bialy for a buck-fifty with a free side of raw onions, tomatoes, and capers. Next, order a side of cream cheese for fifty cents and a bottomless coffee for two bucks. When the waiter isn't looking, take out the tinfoil crumple of Acme fish that's been sweating in your front pocket, unwrap it, stick it on the bread, lather it in cream cheese, and pile it high with free fixings. The waiter will never be able to detect the salty contraband on your bagel. And if they accuse you of smuggling in lox, start ranting that all fish is illegal. Ever heard of over-fishing?!

Pills on the Table

Nothing goes together quite like sable and blood pressure medication. Sprinkle a little Benazepril into your egg cream and swill it like a champ. You're the boss. Even if the morning routine only calls for fosinopril and a little Colace, plopping an entire bottle of MiraLAX onto the table is a sign of power and virility. It's your right to show off in public. Let people know how much Metamucil you can handle in one sitting. Waiters and passersby should know exactly the kind of fella they're dealing with when they give you that extra basket of bialys. Pass the Prinivil!

Katz's Delicatessen

FOUNDED: 1888 by the Iceland Brothers

STATS: Banishing around 200 Old Jewish Men per year for protesting the price of pastrami, serving tourists hundreds of tons worth of treif, a few five-buck hot dogs, and a shipping container of salami to the boys in the army

PASTRAMI PRICE BY THE POUND: $34 (plus a tip for the slicer)

TOP DOG: Jake Dell (aka Junior, he loves that)

UNOFFICIAL MOTTO: "We can charge whatever and they'll still eat here"

TOILET: YES

Hey, Waiter!

Old Jewish Men were understandably upset when Katz's got rid of the waiters. Being served while in a seated position at a table is your right, and futzing around at the deli counter and charming the pastrami slicers is a young man's game. It's not your job to be a circus performer, side-stepping tables and tourists with a tray of hot deli food. You're an Old Yid, not Oscar Robertson.

Lines Are for Suckers

Katz's always has a long line no matter what. Good for them, bad for you. If Katz's wanted to see you on a regular basis, they would institute an OJM VIP system. This is where the OJM Deli Association comes in. If you flash your membership card, you should be prioritized to the front of the line. How about a little respect? If you do happen to get stuck on line, this is a wonderful opportunity to complain to the person next to you.

Packed with Morons

Fifty years ago, the Greater OJM Community of the Lower East Side voted Katz's Deli the "best place to get a bowl of soup and sit in the neighborhood." But these days, the place is clogged with indecisive bozo tourists who don't carry cash to tip the countermen slicers. It's about time Katz's put a cap on all the out-of-towners or gave them an up-charge. And the worst thing about these people? The endless reenactments of the scene from *When Harry Met Sally* while you're trying to clog your arteries as fast as possible. If you wanted to be reminded of how long its been since you've given a woman an orgasm, you'd just ask your wife.

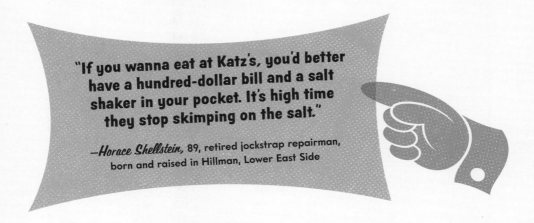

"If you wanna eat at Katz's, you'd better have a hundred-dollar bill and a salt shaker in your pocket. It's high time they stop skimping on the salt."

—*Horace Shellstein*, 89, retired jockstrap repairman, born and raised in Hillman, Lower East Side

Acceptable Conversation at Katz's

----

1. "The tables are too close together."

2. "It's a decent serving, at least."

3. "How much do you think pastrami slicers make a year?"

4. "How much business do you think they do in one day?"

5. "Can you believe they put that schmuck on the wall?"

6. "Sid died."

7. "What's your resting heart rate?"

8. "Second Avenue is better."

DANI LUV'S KATZ'S ORDER

The sixtysomething maestro is famous for having performed at Sammy's Roumanian Steakhouse for over twenty years. Here's Dani's order at Katz's:

"I don't eat much meat anymore—that's a joke, *haha*. Look at me. No, but if I do, I'll drop dead. Katz's—what a wonderful business. Can you believe the line? It's the best fucking pastrami in the world and I love it, but I can't resist chopped liver. That's my thing, but I don't do it anymore. I keep kosher and Katz's isn't kosher. So it's a little bit sad, but at Katz's I eat a tuna sandwich. Cold tuna and a Dr. Brown's Cream Soda."

Zabar's

FOUNDED: 1934 by Lillian and Louis Zabar

STATS: Saul Zabar threatens to sue at least ten customers a year, half of them family members, for looking at him the wrong way; buying and selling at least one Upper West Side block each decade and then forgetting what they own; selling a boatload of coffee (yes, these are precise statistics)

PRICE OF NOVA LOX BY THE POUND: $64 (before haggling)

UNOFFICIAL MOTTO: "It's more than a grocery store, g-ddammit"

TOILET: NOT A CHANCE, PAL (rumors swirling about burgeoning toilets on the mezzanine)

Deli? Grocery Store? Eh, Whateva!

Zabar's is a magnificent all-in-one. Most people think of the grocery store or the bizarre selection of appliances when they hear the name Zabar's, but the café is where the deli magic happens. It was built to accommodate Old Jewish Men who struggle with sore feet and can't complete an entire shopping trip without getting jazzed up on coffee. Zabar's grocery is one of the only places in the universe worth traveling more than twenty minutes from your house. But, sure, make a fuss about it—twenty minutes is twenty minutes.

This Better Be Worth It

Out-of-state weddings—why bother? Some restaurant you've never heard of—what's so great about it? The new bagel place down the street—you think I've never had a bagel before? Exercise—sure, I lift food into my mouth every day. Old Jewish Men need to know that The Ask is worth The Schlep. Any place that a fella hasn't heard of before requires a detailed explanation for why it's better than something geographically closer. OJM don't schlep for deli, but Zabar's is unusual—it has items you can't get elsewhere. The verdict: Worth the schlep.

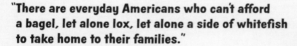

NADLER'S CORNER: NOSHING IN CONGRESS

"There are everyday Americans who can't afford a bagel, let alone lox, let alone a side of whitefish to take home to their families."

—*Bernie Sanders*, most likely

When Congress won't provide a good spread, you gotta bring your own. Schlepping a jumbo bag of smelly fish and other oily deli food from the Upper West Side is what Old Jewish Men call real politickin'. Doesn't matter if someone's getting inaugurated, impeached, executed, or giving testimony about the future of democracy—you're gonna need a big spread for the big day. No sharing.

Only congressional aides and the innermost circle at OJM HQ know what Representative Jerrold Nadler (D-NY) had in the Zabar's bag he brought onto the House floor during impeachment hearings in 2021. But according to a few expert witnesses, Jerry doesn't leave Zabar's without at least two chocolate babkas, a pound of whitefish, half a dozen bagels, and a quarter pound of belly lox. How else does one expect to prolong life?

How to PLACATE OJM, Deli-Style

by SAM LERNER, actor on *The Goldbergs*

MY FATHER, KEN LERNER, is motivated by one thing and one thing only: Jewish deli food. In the past when I've needed a favor from him, something like babysitting my dog or getting my mail/packages when I'm out of town, or even just asking him to scoot over on the couch, pastrami is a tool I've kept in my tool belt. Specifically Langer's in Los Angeles, but Ken accepts most forms of pastrami payment.

I'm not sure what it is about that smoked meat, but it literally moves mountains. "Dad, can you help me with a self-tape?" "Take me to lunch." "Dad, can you help me with my taxes?" "Take me to lunch." "Dad, I think I'm gonna propose to my girlfriend. Any tips?" "I'll tell you over lunch—on you." I'm not sure if this works on other dads. It could just be my own, but I can almost guarantee this is a universal thing. So if you take away one thing from this, it's that you should always present Old Jewish Men with a peace offering if you want something done, and that offering is salty cured beef.

"Well, I'm not sure about their cart exactly, but if someone asks you for the 'nishes' instead of the knishes, you know what you're dealing with. That said, we welcome all shapes and sizes of gentiles and whatever pronunciation they choose to use, as long as the check clears."

—*Willie Zabar*, fourth-generation Zabar, on how to spot a gentile at his store

Barney Greengrass, "The Sturgeon King"

FOUNDED: 1908 by Barney Greengrass

MONTHLY SALES STATS: 8 million pounds of blintzes, an entire school of fish, 10,000 pounds of sturgeon, one sliced raw onion

PRICE OF STURGEON BY THE POUND: $69 (minus the thumb on the scale)

UNOFFICIAL MOTTO: "Still kicking, but not high"

TOILET: YES

Gimme the Belly Lox

If you don't live in New York, hopefully one day soon you will make your pilgrimage to the best sittery in the world, Barney Greengrass. Barney's well-preserved room was designed as an oasis for Old Jewish Men and has everything you could ever want: seasoned waiters who are openly hostile to naïf youngsters, bottomless coffee served with cold high-quality cream, a decent bathroom with a soft—albeit reliable—flush, and the saltiest, fattiest belly lox in town. There's even a pay phone that works, even though no one pays the bill.

OWNER GARY GREENGRASS ON . . .

PRICES: "You want a pile of shit somewhere else or do you wanna eat at Barney Greengrass?"

BEING A MYTHIC FIGURE: "It's called an entrée, the thing I have. This legacy. My last name. Being a Greengrass is a thing, but I don't use the entrée. My wife and son can use it, but I don't need it."

Honor and Loyalty

The more dedicated you are to a place like Barney Greengrass, the more loyalty they will give you in return. After decades of lounging there all day every day, your order will be ready by the time you arrive. Don't expect a free breakfast, but eventually you will start to notice things going your way: a few extra napkins, a clean fork, an additional egg in the scramble, even the occasional complimentary orange juice top off. The sky's the limit.

Getting in Bed with Barney

When the doc gives you a clean bill of health, it's time to celebrate. Forget strip clubs—this is the place to cheat. Barney Greengrass is a quick ride from Mount Sinai hospital, and now that you've got those great numbers on paper, order whatever the hell you want. Eggs and onions, orange juice, blintzes, borscht, bagel and lox. Celebrate today, drop dead tomorrow. You only die once.

AT BARNEY GREENGRASS

"The Woolworth Building was the tallest building in the world for thirty years, not twenty years. I don't know what dumpster you get your information from."

◇◇◇◇◇◇◇◇◇◇◇◇◇◇◇◇◇◇◇◇◇◇◇◇◇◇◇

"You know Richard Kind comes in here. We ate together once."
"He invited you?"
"He was at the table next to me."

◇◇◇◇◇◇◇◇◇◇◇◇◇◇◇◇◇◇◇◇◇◇◇◇◇◇◇

"The coffee's no good here."
"I can't even taste it.
I can't taste anything anymore."
[takes a sip] "You know, you're right. Neither can I."

THE WAITERS: "Things are done here on an informal basis. We want to be efficient and somewhat friendly. We try to be friendly. You know, there's times you can schmooze and there's times when we're too busy."

LETTING OLD JEWISH MEN SIT AROUND DRINKING COFFEE ALL DAY: "They're pretty intuitive. They know when it's time to wrap it up. You know, sometimes you gotta hit the gong and get 'em out of here."

(Non-New York)

DELI

ASSOCIATION-

RATED ESTABLISHMENTS

THESE ARE THE UP-AND-COMERS, THE FARM-TEAM AAA affiliates of the OJM major leagues. Don't get us wrong, these guys hit hard, but not quite hard enough to be top tier. Add a more powerful flush, improved coffee-waiter circulation, and softer seats, and they might get there. Or they could just move to New York.

(Don't worry, we reevaluate every forty-eight years.)

Schwartz's Deli

FOUNDED: 1928 by Reuben Schwartz

LOCATION: Montreal, Canada

STATS: A boatload of smoked meat sold, over one million hot dogs served (side-loaded with choux, of course)

UNOFFICIAL MOTTO: "Just because we're not in New York doesn't mean we can't yell at you over the counter."

TOILET: YES

Long Live Reuben

Who was Reuben Schwartz? Apparently, he was a heartless asshole who embezzled money, gambled away profits, and hired underage kids he could work to the bone for practically nothing. Sometimes that's just what it takes to get a business off the ground. After nearly torpedoing the place a couple of times, Reuben was eventually bailed out by some musician. (When a musician has to save you financially, you know you're in deep shit.) All of that aside, you gotta give Reuben Schwartz a pass, for he founded one of the greatest delis in North America.

A Testament to the Sandwich's Quality

Rumor has it that when sax king John Zorn was in town for a Jazz Fest gig and got a subpar, imitation smoked meat sandwich instead of his rider-requested Schwartz's, he threw the phony sandwich at the hotel wall and refused to go on until Jazz Fest founder André Ménard personally fetched and delivered the authentic grub. That's how good Schwartz's sandwiches are. As an Old Jewish Man, you're entitled to throw any sandwich at any wall at any time for any reason, especially if your wife made it.

The ROADSIDE REUBEN

by ELLIOT SATENSTEIN, OJM Bostonian

YOU WON'T MIND hitting the road between New York and Boston since it means a stop at Rein's Deli off I-84 in Vernon, Connecticut. Whoever opened the place knew exactly what they were doing. Who knows if Rein's could make it as a New York City deli, but it doesn't matter. The guy who understood that OJM will pull over for decent (not out-of-this-world) deli instead of some crappy side-of-the-road joint had the right idea. What a smart location. They have all the classics: edible sours/half-sours, above-average corned beef, and rugelach that does the trick. It's safe to say that Rein's has the best everything in a forty-mile radius. However, they're closed on Christmas—what's the deal with that?

Zaftigs Delicatessen

FOUNDED: 5757

LOCATION: Brookline, Massachusetts

STATS: A few plates of matzo brai served every Passover along with a hulking side of Canadian bacon

UNOFFICIAL MOTTO: "Jewish Enough for Brookline"

TOILET: YES

DELI ASSOCIATION · APPROVAL PENDING

No Bagel Chips and Cream Cheese?

Ever since Rubin's—a nice kosher deli down the street in "Baruchline"—closed, people have been going to Zaftigs. What other choice do they have? (Answer: Michael's, another good deli just down the street.) The thing about Zaftigs is that they used to give every table complimentary bagel chips and cream cheese. These days? You gotta ask for it. Sign of the times, eh? To their credit, without trusty ol' Zaftigs it'd be a one-deli town, so let's hope they stick around—at least until Michael's gets more tables. Zaftigs giveth and Zaftigs taketh away.

> "The first time I had lobster I thought I was having an allergic reaction or hemorrhaging it tasted so good—it was the closest I ever got to seeing God."
>
> —*Rich Goldberg,* 73, social studies teacher

Nate'n Al's

FOUNDED: 1945 by Nate Rimer and Al Mendelson

LOCATION: Los Angeles, California

STATS: Many breakfast bagels, some corned beef hash, and all of Larry King's wives served

UNOFFICIAL MOTTO: "The food is average, but who cares—we're famous"

TOILET: YES

DELI ASSOCIATION APPROVAL PENDING

But Is It Any Good?

Opened by two friends from Detroit, the famous Nate'n Al's is one of the oldest kosher-style delis in California. Despite looking a little crappy from the outside, and having a pretty nothing interior too, the joint has been a known meeting place for Hollywood personalities like Nancy Sinatra, Kareem Abdul-Jabbar, Lew Wasserman, Michael Jackson, and Neil Diamond. It's true that Larry King bought his house in Beverly Hills to be closer to Nate 'n Al's, but these days the jury is out on whether the food is any good. Said former New Yorker and current OJM Ken Lerner: "I recently had a nice pastrami sandwich and my wife got eggs. She keeps kosher, so I had to watch her eat eggs. Nothing sexy about watching your wife eat eggs."

Pepto-Bismol

FOR UPSET STOMACH INDIGESTION NAUSEA

8 FL OZ

Controls common DIARRHEA

THE POWER OF *Langer's*

by JASON DIAMOND, **writer**

WHEN YOU FIND A GREAT DELI, you should cherish it. They're a dying thing because people are concerned that if they eat a corned beef sandwich every now and then that their heart will explode because they had an uncle named Morris who had a coronary back in 1976 that the family still talks about. What they don't talk about is that Uncle Morris smoked several cigars a day and ran on pure stress about his business failing and his wife always yelling at him. Top it off with multiple cured meat sandwiches a week, and sure, no ticker is going to survive that. But the thing is that a great pastrami sandwich every now and then is good for you. It brings you joy. And while there's really no beating Katz's in New York, there's something about Langer's in Los Angeles. It looks great and the vibe is unbeatable. But what's best about it is that you can just sit.

Drink some coffee, and make sure you drink at least two glasses of water to rehydrate. The most important thing, though, is you can digest. Digesting is an art. It's like Jewish meditation. You sit there and you let your stomach do its thing while you think about life and the sandwich you just ate. It's hard to do that at Katz's or anywhere in New York City, for that matter. So when you visit L.A., skip the expensive wellness center and go to Langer's. Eat a nice sandwich, then sit there, breathe, and think about how great you have it.

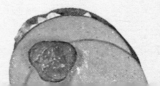

The OJM Deli Association . . . and More

The Coffee Shop

SITTING FOR HOURS

*"Cream should be cold, not room-temperature or hot.
Cream goes into coffee—not whole milk,
not skim milk, not two-percent. Cream and that's it.
Not a lot of cream, just a little cream."*

—*Hillel*, son of Gamaliel III, younger brother of Judah II, in Judea (before 280 BCE)

WITHOUT A GOOD coffee shop, Old Jewish Men are lost in their own neighborhood. Why? Because a coffee shop can also be a sittery, which is defined as a place for "being left alone to sit," and is often where you will go after eating lunch at home but still want coffee and space to relax.

Most diners and luncheonettes, by contrast, want to keep the tables moving and will try to give you the boot. If some rookie waiter says you're not ordering enough or have been sitting there too long, then politely explain that you've been "coming here fifty years and I've spent half a million bucks keeping the lights on in this dump!"

OJM COFFEE SHOP NON-EATING ACTIVITIES

reading the paper • day trading • sports betting • taking "meetings"
hitting on the new barista • gossiping about the owner • napping
making loud inane conversation • asking for day-olds when they're still fresh

Booths Over Chairs

Always take the booth. Don't listen to the waitstaff when they lie that booths are only for groups of two or more. It's your right to sit all day at a booth by yourself nursing a single cup of drip coffee (that you brought from home, of course). The chairs at coffee shops are too hard, and their backrests are too soft. Pro tip: Never sit on a stool of any kind, especially if it spins—they're dangerous and will hurt your back and the restaurant won't pay to reconstruct your vertebrae. If there's leather, take it. If there's only a wood chair available, and some young pisher is camped out on a leather seat, yell at them until they give it up. It's their fault for sitting there in the first place.

Eggs Should Never Be Microwaved

There's a lot that can go wrong at a coffee shop: microwaved eggs, room-temperature cream, stinky or clogged toilets (probably from you), waitstaff claiming that even *they* don't have a place to go (always a lie—so where are they unloading?), silty and overpriced coffee that sits around all day, no outlets to charge your pager, uncomfortable seats, slow baristas, overly chatty baristas, rude baristas who don't wanna chat for an hour about acid reflux. But at the end of the day, it's not about what they do or don't have, it's about finding a way to gripe about it.

Café Table Service

The GREATEST SCAM EVER PERPETRATED on OJM

by E.Z. RINSKY, novelist

1713. EUROPE. Western civilization is getting enlightened. Rats aren't carrying quite as many diseases. Someone has finally figured out that steam can power machines other than baths. And most importantly, there's coffee. The sharpest minds turn to the obvious question: How to monetize Austria's newfound java addiction?

Early coffeehouses are financially untenable. Old Jewish Men abuse the business model: They fill up a mug from the samovar, and then loiter for hours. Finally, a sharp entrepreneur named Solomon Weiss—a blossoming OJM himself—cracks the code. When the OJM arrive at Weiss' Café on a brisk December morning, they're met by a smiling hostess.

"Please sit down. Someone will be right with you."

The confused OJM take seats at a small round table. A young, nice-smelling woman holding a pad and pen materializes at their table.

"What can I getcha?" she asks.

The dumbfounded OJM order: "Espresso with a shtickle of cold milk on the side and the biggest Danish you have!"

After the waitress retreats to the kitchen, one particularly feeble OJM notes that the server laid a hand on his shoulder. "She's interested!" he insists. Society is not yet familiar with the concept of working for tips.

Initially, the breakfast is one of the finest the OJM have ever enjoyed: *Refill on coffee, dear! Hey—another "round of hot buns for all my friends!"* But after half an hour, Weiss himself emerges from the kitchen to deliver the coup de grâce: "Gentlemen, I'm afraid we need that table now."

The OJMs shift uncomfortably. They can sense they've been had. One inspects the bill through his bifocals. His face creases in consternation as he reads the line at the bottom. Service nicht inbegriffen it says—service not included.

"Fellas . . ." he whispers. "We're in trouble."

Toileting at a Coffee Shop

What do you call a coffee shop without a toilet? A scam. How can a business serve diuretics all day and claim they don't have a can? The nerve of these baristas to peddle this nonsense. Here's a solution: Instead of a ten-punch coffee card that scores a free cup of joe, what if it scored a sweet number two? Most Old Jewish Men know that every coffee joint, no matter what they say, has a working john somewhere on the premises. So if you gotta go, march right in like you own the place and get right to work. If they ask where you're going say, "No palo Anglaisia." A barista has gotta be out of their mind to stop you from using that commode. Don't get in an Old Jewish Man's way.

> "I place no limit on the amount of coffee I can drink. I allow myself an infinite amount and I like it hot with cream. Sometimes cappuccino, sometimes Americano, but nothing fancier than that."
>
> —*Jerry Seinfeld*

TIPPING RUBRIC

1. If the barista steams milk to make your beverage, you SHOULD tip at least a buck.

2. For a hot drip coffee, canned beverage, or an iced coffee to go, you are NOT REQUIRED to tip.

3. If you stay at the coffee shop for longer than ten minutes you SHOULD tip a buck. This includes using the bathroom, making phone calls, or hitting on the barista.

Caffe Reggio: The Last of a Dying Breed

Despite the hordes of sniveling NYU students on Hinge dates and loud, clueless tourists, Caffe Reggio is the last tolerable sittery for Old Jewish Men of the Village. As an OJM trainee, you belong there. Reggio is the only place north of Houston Street* that plays classical music at a reasonable volume where you can sit all day reading your six-hundred-page book about the origins of the mustard seed and not worry about getting hassled by the staff.

On any given day, Old Jewish academics and neighborhood Bohemians cram into the back of the café to drill Americanos, clamp their gums around stale biscotti, and complain openly about the coffee and the most overpaid administrators at NYU. It's important to gloat about how you're still tenured, despite having not done any work for a decade. Another round of cannoli, signor!

* It's a fact. Try reading a map!

The Great Lower East Side Coffee Shop Migration

OJM

An OJM Fable

TURN THE PAGE AND THE JOURNEY SHALL BEGIN . . . .

THE EARLY 2010S CE SAW A MIGRATION OF Old Jewish Men on the Lower East Side that shook the neighborhood. For years, OJM gathered at Roots & Vines, a small, family-owned coffee shop near the corner of Grand and Clinton Streets. As recalled by longtime customer Bernie Osofsky, "That place had it all. Great tables, comfortable chairs, a sturdy can, and reliable air circulation."

Fellas like Osofsky remember Roots & Vines as an oasis where hordes of listless Old Jewish Men could loiter, drink the same cup of coffee all day, and cash in on the high-speed internet to trade stocks or stream hours of summer-afternoon sports.

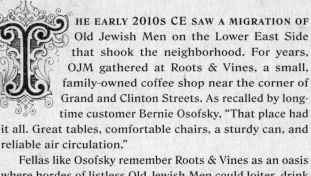

"Then it all changed," explains Josh Seigel, seventy-nine, another longtime customer.

In 2012, Roots & Vines closed its doors without warning, leaving the OJM stranded and coffee shop–less. "It's not like we were gonna cross Delancey to a different joint," Arthur Finer grumbles. "It's a dangerous intersection."

Miraculously, a few months after the closure, a whitewalled hipster coffee shop called Pushcart Coffee popped up. Within seconds of opening its doors, the nine-seat shop was flooded with dusty local Old Jewish Men. The grumpy globs came in hungry and thirsty, desperate for high-pressure toilets and a place to sit.

"It was an assault," recalls Jeremy Coleman, a divorced forty-year-old Pushcart barista. "They would ask what kind of yogurt we use and then demand to see the container, but never buy it. You can't run a business like that."

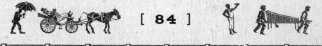

What happened next is the greatest fear of every OJM with an enlarged prostate: Pushcart shuttered bathroom access, citing "leakage." Few knew what was coming, and as OJM Moshe Wilkominski remembers it, "They covered up the power outlets and that was it. Game over. No more day trading. There was no more money coming in." A week later, Pushcart would even take the draconian measure of replacing comfortable chairs with hard, unforgiving benches.

"The Pushcart execs knew our lower backs couldn't take the stiffness of those seats," Howard Zimmerman recalls. "We protested by staying even longer than usual—sometimes we'd sit there from morning until night, but our bodies couldn't take it. It put Sammy Gelman in the hospital."

Pushcart Coffee would soon open a second location in Gramercy and within months would close the Lower East Side shop. The Lower East Side suffered its worst coffee shop drought in more than a century.

But then, something incredible happened: The owners of Ost Cafe in the East Village saw an opportunity to cash in. "We understood the risks," admits one Ost Cafe investor when asked about the Old Jewish Men problem. "That's why we got a double-plated toilet and an extra fuse for the bathroom fan."

In 2015, Ost opened on Grand Street, just a ten-minute waddle from the old Pushcart location. Shortly thereafter, the great migration was complete.

"The place is decent," shrugs Harris Gurny, an Old Jewish Man of zero notoriety. "So I go."

STEPPIN' OUT: A Weekly City-by-City Guide

	MONDAY	TUESDAY	WEDNESDAY
DETROIT	**The Schvitz.** Best heat in the Midwest. Go in the evening and bring vodka. Tell Paddy and the Russian "hi."	**Zingerman's Creamery.** Worth the schlep from Motown to Ann Arbor.	**John King Books.** Not enough books on maintaining brisket moistness, but the prices are good.
LONDON	**Platters Deli.** Unapologetic and surprisingly good apple pie for a classic deli.	**Panzer's Deli.** Don't sleep on the baked goods. The Zabar's of the UK.	**Golds Menswear.** Only the finest silks. Good value shoes.
LOS ANGELES	**California Polo Club.** Pricey, but this is where deals are done and careers are made.	**Courage Bagels.** Ask for Moss and buy an OJM & Courage shirt while you're at it.	**Factor's Famous Deli.** In the Jewish heart of the city. Food is good, but the atmosphere is better. Good blintzes.
MIAMI/BOCA	**Zak the Baker.** Don't be fooled by the strange façade; the babka is good and moist.	**Fontainebleau.** Lounge by the pool and imagine you're Don Rickles sitting next to Sinatra for a night.	**Miami Beach Golf Club.** Schmooze your way into some beachfront property.
NEW YORK	**JG Melon.** Always crowded. Bring quarters for the jukebox. Great key lime pie.	**Club Macanudo.** The cigars are fresh, great after a night at JG.	**Russian & Turkish Baths.** Get a punch card. Don't forget to eat lunch. Never go on coed days.
PARIS	**L'As du Fallafel.** Go in the offseason. Sweet-talk your way to the front of the line and make sure they don't skimp on the tahini.	**Chez XU.** Forget all the steak frites, the best food in Paris is Chinese food. Stay close to home on this one.	**Chez Prune.** Sit outside facing the canal for hours chain-smoking cigars and eating buttered baguette.
PHILLY	**Schlesinger's.** The tuna Reuben might be the sandwich of the future.	**Famous 4th Street Deli.** Get the big bowl of soup and shut up.	**Benjamin Franklin Museum.** Life is a kind of chess . . . if you want to save $5, the outside views of the house and fountain are free.

THURSDAY	FRIDAY	SATURDAY	SUNDAY
Motown Museum. Learn about why Detroit used to matter.	**Detroit Institute of Bagels.** Does the job. Good portions, get in early. Never go on weekends.	**Baker's Keyboard Lounge.** Go for the music. Bring your own food. Expect to pay for parking.	**Detroit Zoo.** The penguin exhibit is worth the trip. Don't stick out your hand.
New Docklands Steam Club. Solid heat and steam, good towels, bad location but worth it.	**Carmelli Bakery.** Don't leave without a warm challah.	**Ronnie Scott's.** Captivating, and not too loud. Go on a night when there's a trio. Never order cocktails.	**Cigar Terrace at the Wellesley.** Will make you forget who you are for at least a few hours. A cigar and Perrier go well together.
Mort's Deli. The best rye bread, onion rolls, and chopped herring.	**Brentwood Country Club.** Good place to schmooze for business. This place runs on favors. Have cigars in your pockets.	**Formosa Cafe.** Hollywood hangout of the past with Szechuan food that still packs a punch.	**Craig's.** Where deals used to happen; the food is still decent.
Century Grill. Good portions of brisket, but push them to put ribs on the menu.	**Harding Avenue.** Sit out here and judge people—who's eating the most expensive steak tonight?	**The Shul.** Always a minyan. Bring your grandson and get him a job.	**Mo's Bagels & Deli.** Everything's good except the potato pancakes. Sit inside for hours. Nice bagels.
The Lock Museum. Make an appointment and browse for hours. Some of the most original bathrooms in the city.	**Pietro's.** Don't be fooled by the Italian food, this place is packed with OJM. Just look at the plaques on the walls.	**Mr. Wonton.** This is where deals are made in Park Slope. Always fresh, a good corner view of the avenue.	**Liebman's Deli.** Still kosher. The last deli in the Bronx. Get the chopped liver.
Jardin du Luxembourg. It's nice watching the youngsters push the boats around with sticks.	**Le Club Barrière Paris.** It's good to roll the dice a little bit. Take a load off and bring a stack of cash.	**Shakespeare and Company.** Go upstairs where it's quietest. If there's someone on the piano, make sure they're good. If they're not, complain.	**Sacha Finkelsztajn.** Grab a vatrushka, 'nuff said.
Steve Stein's Famous Deli. Surprisingly good cinnamon rolls, authentic and dirty in a good way.	**Masonic Temple.** Go see what all the fuss is about.	**The Mütter Museum.** Free entry. Ever wonder what a gallbladder looks like up close? How about a large intestine?	**Two Robbers Fishtown.** Ask for Vik. He'll show you what's what.

SAFE TREIF

Chinese Food

**"There are three things Jewish people worship:
God, compound interest, and egg foo young."**

—Alan Greenspan, quite possibly

BACK IN THE DAY, the Chinese restaurant represented a place where Jews went to escape the mentality of the old country. These joints felt sophisticated. Old Jewish Men weren't always welcome in Italian restaurants, and all those crucifixes on the walls and butter-soaked sausage was a little much. Chinese restaurants, on the other hand, were the perfect compromise: a heimish yet cosmopolitan experience that didn't feel taboo.

There's nothing that says *Assimilated Jew* like counting shrimp to make sure they didn't give you fewer than last time while guzzling tongue-singeing green tea. The best thing? At Chinese restaurants you don't have to worry about getting a stomachache because there's hardly any dairy (just stay away from the crab rangoon!). Chinese American food has the perfect salty-to-fried-to-meaty-to-sweet-and-spicy ratio that other food groups just can't compete with.

IF FORTUNE COOKIES WERE WRITTEN FOR OLD JEWISH MEN

1. An incredible bowel movement is coming your way

2. A faithful diuretic is a welcome friend

3. Smile once in a while and you might get more free tea

4. Ignore chest pain, it's all in your head

5. Be wary of those who ask you to schlep

6. You'll never get better at golf

7. You still have to tip, even though it's Christmas

Pork? Chicken? Who Cares!

Sure, Chinese restaurants are open on Christmas, which is all well and good. But here's the real reason Old Jewish Men love Chinese food: plausible deniability. Bite into a sparerib and not sure if it's pork or chicken? What's the difference?* It doesn't count as breaking kosher if it happens at a Chinese restaurant. During the course of your experience at Joe's Shanghai, it's your job to stick a fork (OJM have no idea how to use chopsticks) into every plate on the table so that by the end of the meal your sleeve drips with sweet sauce. Just eat everything in sight and enjoy.

* According to Rabbi Yehuda Goldstein, the Gemara teaches us that a sparerib is not always "what it appears to be." This comes from the line in Bereshit: "A rib is not always a rib, a thigh not always a thigh, a chicken is not always a fish nor a fish a chicken."

CHINESE RESTAURANT OVER/UNDERS

O/U 1 time asking for a fork

O/U 4 seat changes

O/U 8 cups of complimentary tea

O/U 4 times reaching across table to poach from other eaters' plates

O/U 4 times asking how the hell you're supposed to eat with chopsticks

O/U 2 times demanding a different fortune

Ordering Is Half the Fun

The best part about eating at a Chinese restaurant is arguing with everyone at the table about what you want. Egg rolls? Of course! Chicken? Obviously. Beef? Why not. Pork? Well, only if you pretend it's chicken. The main thing is to eat everything that's on your plate and a bit of what's on everybody's else's. Seconds? Sure, order more. It's cheap!

"It should be called the 'lunch combination' — there's nothing special about it. They think they can just mush the chicken and rice together on the same plate and give you a can of cheap soda with a bowl of last night's soup. Gimme a break. It's a combination. But if I were them, I'd do the exact same thing."

—*Syd Cohen,* 82, Public Relations, on the Lunch Special

With Such Prices, Who Needs to Cook?

To be considered a great deal, a Chinese lunch special MUST offer not only soup and a can of seltzer but also a healthy portion of food and a fortune cookie. A "healthy portion" is defined by the Three-Quarters Dinner Rule: The helping must be at least three-quarters of the dinner special's size and any less is a rip-off.

Don't let them think they can get away with serving half as much food for half the price. That's not a deal. It is written in the OJM Chinese Food Lunch Special Treatise that "Old Jewish Men shall go right to the source of the three-quarters problem," and to "embark on a hostile conversation with whoever's in charge" if the lunch special doesn't meet this requirement. But when it comes down to it, even if it's a little skimpy and still under ten bucks, why cook?

Sacred Chow

There are only a handful of phone numbers you should have memorized: 911, Hatzalah (they resuscitate for free), and at least a few Chinese delivery spots. Despite knowing these restaurant numbers by heart, you should still have

the menus taped to your refrigerator over pictures of your family, just in case. If anyone asks where you order from, give them the runaround. The more people who have this number, the longer you gotta wait for your food. It's all about getting your chow as quickly as possible.

Pictured: Sid and Gary keep the tradition alive.

The Pre-Wonton Christmas Shvitz

It is highly recommended to shvitz for at least three hours on Christmas morning to maximize fried wonton intake at that evening's feast. By depleting your body of sodium, you will need to make up for it by doubling or even tripling the normal amount of soy sauce eaten on a normal day. It's hard work, but someone's gotta do it, and this is an old Jew's solemn duty on Christmas.

If an OJM eats something other than Chinese food on Christmas, he can expect to receive a strongly worded letter from the Greater OJM Community Executive Board that could lead to dismissal. Christmas is when the OJM community gets together to honor the savior of MSG, Hymie Kungpaostein, and brag about how every Christmas song was written by Jews. Respek, Irving Berlin.

GREATER OJM COMMUNITY GUIDELINES INFRACTION
- -

DEAR MELVIN WIZNITZER,

What were you doing at a Greek restaurant on Christmas Day? We saw you shuffle out of your apartment in a stained Brandeis sweatshirt with the hood pulled up. You think we don't recognize that barrel-like gait? You look like a LEGO. We got plenty of fellas with a lot more hip rotation who make a lot more dough than you and don't feel the need to be so-called free thinkers on the biggest Chinese food night of the year.

This is your one and only warning. If we see you anyplace but a Chinese restaurant or movie theater on Christmas, you're out!

Signed,

OJM COMMUNITY EXECUTIVE BOARD

QUIZ: WHAT JEWISH-COMPOSER-WHO-WROTE-ALL-THE-XMAS-MUSIC ARE YOU?

☑ Black Dress Pants   ☐ Khakis

☑ Thick-Frame Glasses   ☐ Narrow-Frame Glasses

☐ Cigars   ☑ Cigarettes

☑ Piano   ☐ Cello

CONGRATULATIONS!
You came to America at the turn of the
century to escape pogroms, mastered
your instrument in under a year,
composed half of the Great American
Songbook, and died of tuberculosis
before the age of fifty. Your estate
is valued at $200 million.

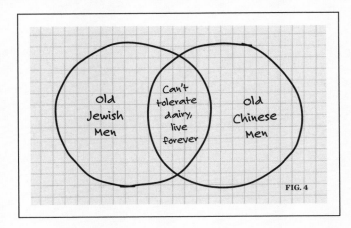

Old Jewish Men   Can't tolerate dairy, live forever   Old Chinese Men

FIG. 4

Soft L.A. West Coasters

"In California, they don't throw their garbage away—they make it into TV shows."

—ANNIE HALL

From shul to pool, these sun-allergic fellas live to pretend they're young but can't remember if they've had eight divorces or eight heart attacks. Although wife-number-who-the-hell-knows said it's time to buy a beachfront place in Malibu, these Old Jewish West Coasters haven't been to the beach in three decades. Why get sand in your shorts when you have an infinity pool?

Soft L.A. OJM are producers, actors, lawyers, "personalities," and media moguls who spend their days getting stretched out by butt-lifted personal trainers/mistresses who keep quiet when sessions are interrupted by the real marathons: consultations with the alimony lawyer, always taken on speakerphone. They're mostly New York runaways who fled for sunnier skies, sport finely trimmed facial hair and expensive Chais (necklaces, not the lattes), and reside in Beverly Hills, Beverlywood, Malibu, and Brentwood. If you're not an old friend, good luck getting them on the horn,

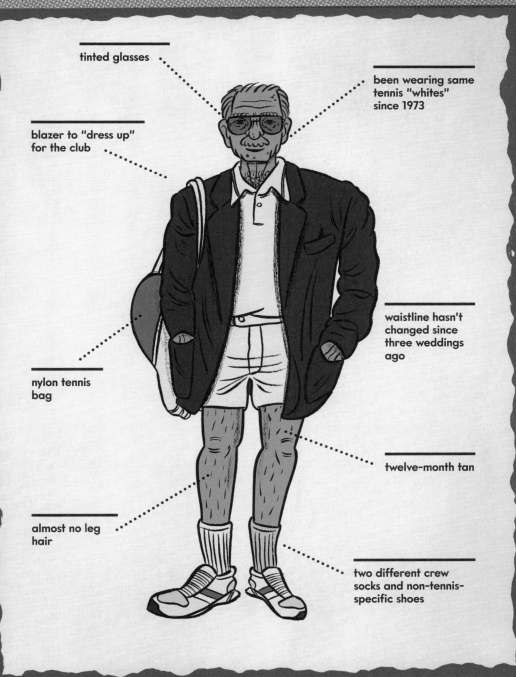

tinted glasses

been wearing same tennis "whites" since 1973

blazer to "dress up" for the club

waistline hasn't changed since three weddings ago

nylon tennis bag

twelve-month tan

almost no leg hair

two different crew socks and non-tennis-specific shoes

because these machers claim to have the busiest schedules on planet Earth. They're mister big-time and they got no time, no time at all! No time for *you*.

These showbiz types know how to produce one good movie and spend the rest of their lives showing it off. What's the point of having status if you can't brag about it? They'd attend the opening of an envelope if there were a chance to drop their own name. In their minds, they're still movers and shakers—even if they can barely walk—and they can't wait to tell you who they worked with back in the day. "Did I ever tell you about the time Sid Caesar borrowed some of my dental floss backstage? Yes? Well, once more then."

All That Assimilatin' Ain't Foolin' Nobody

They think they're slick because they changed their last names but forgot to switch the first. "Seymour Johnson"? Sure, buddy. Nice try. These fellas might have forgotten they're Jewish, but no one else has.

A lot of West Coast OJM have spent the last fifty years sipping artisanal coffee in sunny rooms, falling asleep reading scripts, yelling at judges, flipping leased cars, chatting up Laker Girls, and name-dropping proctologists. Family members back east think they smile too much and are tired of hearing the term "back end." Not a day goes by when these fellas wonder if they could have had the same success in New York. They wear toupees, break ten smoothie blenders a year, and waste thousands on nutritionists, hair follicle experts, and dietitians. But hey, their skin looks pretty shiny. And that's what matters.

The Larry Rub Down

On the other side of Tinseltown are more Soft L.A. fellas, like the late Larry "King" Zeiger, who insist that taking a stroll is exercise. This breed of OJM wears coronaries like a badge of honor, a sign of devotion to a shul in Beverly Hills called Nate 'n Al's. Larry was married nine times; some may say he just didn't believe in premarital sex. (Remember, it's not premarital if you never get married. Write that down, kids.)

West Coasters may have soft hands, but don't be fooled—these street-smart fellas grew up hard and L.A. hasn't completely worn them down. It's no coincidence they're so successful—all they do is work. They hail from religious immigrant parents from neighborhoods like Brighton Beach, Borough Park, and Bensonhurst, where laughs were once currency. They can never truly call L.A. home, even if they've been locals for forty years. The California walk-and-talk ain't great, but it'll have to do because one day they're moving back to New York . . . they swear it!

OBIT by MARTIN A. BIMBERMAN, *L.A. Times*

MR. SOFT L.A. JEW, WHO AS A TEEN-

ager became the most feared bookie in the slums of East Williamsburg, and who later parlayed that canny mastery of his fellow man into Never Die Wellness or Your Money Back, a popular line of bath salts, outdoor mesh slippers, and agave ear cleaner for which he was the model in chief, appearing in television ads poolside using his products, died on Friday inside a tanning salon tanning pod in Los Angeles. He was seventy-five.

His spokeswoman (who is also, according to court documents, his second ex-wife) said that the radioactivity of his corpse should not interrupt plans to scatter his ashes over the home of Mr. Diehard New Yorker, also a former East Williamsburg bookie.

CHAPTER 4

How to Live Forever

Here's the long and short of it: For breakfast, start with three heavily salted fried eggs soaked in ketchup with potatoes, toasted and buttered rye bread, and coffee. For lunch, a roast beef sandwich with sweet potato fries (the Jackie Mason special) and a side of slaw. Then polish the day off with fatty lamb chops and a small salad, washed down with a diet cream soda. This is how Old Jewish Men have been doing it for years, and there's no reason to change it up. Forget all the health write-ups about smoothies and vegetables being good for you—that's all just speculation. OJM either drop dead at fifty-seven or push it to 102 no matter how they treat their bodies. Whether you take your coffee with skim milk or cream, we're all headed to the same place.

In this chapter, we'll look at all the OJM keys to longevity, from golf to shvitzing to conversational conservatism to leisure suits. Some OJM Longevity Scholars believe card shuffling extends life by increasing blood flow to the hands, while others insist that the body shouldn't move at all, ever. Meanwhile, OJM Leisure Scholars have argued for several naps spaced throughout the day, while still others postulate that waking up at two in the morning and going to bed at two in the afternoon (the famed "2–2 schedule") is the only way to prolong existence. All observers can agree, however, that napping while someone else is talking is a guaranteed ticket to vigor and immortality.

Life Hack: Cigars, and Plenty of 'Em

Contrary to every single reputable scientific study showing the dangers of smoking, cigars seem to extend the lives of Old Jewish Men. So if you don't already indulge in the occasional stogie (or seven), you gotta start right away. Just know that there are a few rules:

1. Smoking has been proven to stop constipation in its tracks, so tread carefully.

2. After your first coffee and cigar of the day, try mixing in things like whole-fat cottage cheese, onion soup, and schmaltz to make the afternoon go by even slower.

3. If you choose to suck down more than three cigars a day for over forty years, switch to cigarettes when the doctor says your blood pressure could be a little lower. Cigarettes have less tobacco in them so they're like diet cigars.

13-inch Macanudos are the ultimate life extenders.

Doctor's Orders

It's not high, just higher than last time . . . This is all you need to hear to keep doing exactly what you've been doing for the last sixty years. Research shows that exercise is fine in small amounts, but nothing too strenuous. Don't strain. A light jog is okay, but unnecessary. Futzing around the block is good, but no need to break a sweat. You went to get the newspaper at the bottom of the driveway? That's enough! Lifting? For what? Remember: The heart only has so many beats.

If your doctor objects to the above, feel free to humiliate him by deploying this OJM-approved joke that is guaranteed to fall completely flat:

Q: *What do they call the guy who graduates last in his class from medical school?*

A: Doctor!

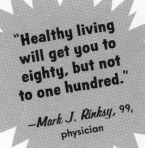

"Healthy living will get you to eighty, but not to one hundred."
—*Mark J. Rinksy,* 99, physician

"Food isn't what kills people. Bad PSA numbers and house fires are what you gotta watch out for."
—*Mussy "The Seed" Moskowitz,* 102, retired roasted nut salesman

Old Gentile Men: A Study in Contrasts

How come old gentile men run ten miles a day, eat nothing but organic greens and grapefruit, never take a puff of anything, and flush money down the crapper on nutritionists, health gurus, and kickboxing classes, all to drop dead at sixty-two? Who knows, but it sure stinks for them. It's a great mystery why health-obsessed gentiles with Viking blood end up with cardiovascular issues and knee problems. Maybe old men are like planes—the bigger the jet, the faster they fly, but the quicker they sputter. After all, ponies live longer than horses.

He's Still Alive?!?

The ridiculous longevity of some Old Jewish Men clearly has less to do with their alarming dietary and shvitzing habits and more to do with other nonquantifiable, almost supernatural factors. Plenty of old men eat like shit and spend several hours a day sweating it out in the steam room, but the shelf life of Old Jewish Men defies logic and science. Maybe the Supreme Leader of the Universe simply counts them among His chosen people. Eh, who knows.

Don't Waste Gestures

At a certain age you will transition from being overly talkative to scarcely conversational. Long explanations become head nods and barely discernible, indirect gesticulations. Regardless of any feelings you might have about Woody Allen, he's a great example of a fella who is physically built to last (small, thin, compact, miserable). Woody went from a Copious Conversationalist in his younger years to a Conversational Conservationist as an OJM. As he's aged, Woody has become increasingly soft-spoken and mortality-obsessed. Sure, a lot of it has to do with certain serious allegations against him, but as an Old Jewish Man, he's a far cry from the fun, talkative fella you used to see on *The Dick Cavett Show*. That's showbiz, folks!

A Few More Gesture Protectors

Jerry Lewis had a similar trajectory. At some point he transitioned from a jocular funnyman into an ornery, tight-lipped OJM. Mel Brooks, however, is a specimen of ancient Old Jewish Man who does not need to conversationally conserve; instead, he energizes himself with abundant and spirited chatter. Some fellas don't feel the need to hold anything in, bankrolling their remaining years by generously giving and taking laughter. Mel is just as lively and fun as ever in his nineties, writing books and making occasional television appearances. Ain't nobody like him.

Friends with the Doc

OJM Hall of Famers like Mel Brooks, Norman Lear, Norman Mailer, Carl Icahn, Jackie Mason, Armand Hammer, George Burns, and Elie Wiesel wouldn't have lived to be ancient without being best friends with their physicians, who also happened to be Old Jewish Men. The reason, however, has nothing to do with access to the latest treatments or medical knowledge—it's because it puts you at ease. How else are you supposed to relax during a blood pressure reading? And more importantly, if the doc ain't a pal, why would you let him stick his sweaty finger up your tuchus? Honorary OJM shoutout to John F. Kennedy, who knew how to work the pill pushers like the best of 'em.

KEY VOCAB

Conversational conservationist: a self-preservation technique believed to extend life by limiting needless chitchat. The idea is that you only get so many words in your lifetime, and there's no point in wasting them talking about the weather.

Copious conversationalist: a self-preservation technique believed to extend life by excessive pontification. Ex: *"How about this rainstorm?"*

BREAKFAST THOUGHTS

Look at Mel's friend Norman Lear, who was singing and working on his show *Breakfast Thoughts* right up until he passed away in 2023 at the age of 101. He was a young man! Norman went on the air once a week to give precious life advice using his camera phone. Here is what he said on his one hundredth birthday:

My breakfast thought at the moment . . . is the moment. Every person who is seeing me now, some are seeing me within months of seeing this or years after seeing this, but whenever all of you are seeing it, that will be the moment you're seeing it. Because this is the moment I'm saying it. What that means to me is living in the moment. The moment between past and present. The moment between after and next. The hammock in the middle between past and present. Treasure it. Use it with love.

Don't Train, Don't Strain

Old Jewish Men do not run marathons. They watch them on television. Who can understand people who do these horrible things to their body? Why run so far if you have no place to go? You're just going in a circle. Physical exertions like

running and skiing and Ironman competitions are suicidal. Let Jim Johnson drop dead at the finish line; you got enough problems. Mo Meyers belongs in front of the tube with a tuna sandwich. Don't be the fella who thinks he's prolonging life by running thirty miles at the age of seventy-five.

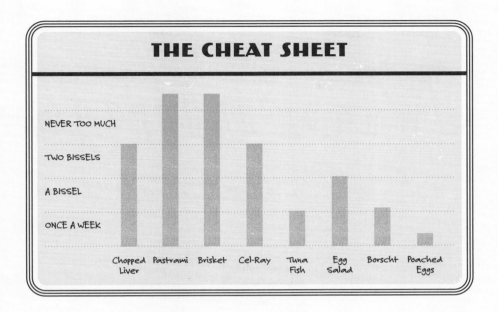

THE CHEAT SHEET

NEVER TOO MUCH

TWO BISSELS

A BISSEL

ONCE A WEEK

Chopped Liver · Pastrami · Brisket · Cel-Ray · Tuna Fish · Egg Salad · Borscht · Poached Eggs

Shuckle Like a Champ

Old Jewish Men are built to sit and can do so for long hours. If you don't think it's true, just look at all the fellas bent over their Talmuds at 770 Eastern Parkway in Crown Heights. Any day of the week you'll see countless, nearly identical Old Jewish Men alternating between shuckling and sitting (or arguing and standing) with their learning partner, a practice called *chevruta*. The ability to curl over a prayer book for uninterrupted twelve-hour stretches is a form of generational stamina. It's all in the hips.

> "Moses was big on stretching after a long day of shuckling. We used to give him hell for it, but honestly it's what got us out of Egypt. Those loose hips of his."
>
> —*Gil Goffer*, age unknown, Hartford, CT

Mornings
Sit Up and Dawdle

THE FIRST FUTZ OF THE day shall commence with ten mindless minutes of moseying around the house and stretching the arms a bit to get the blood going. Then it's time to start wolfing pills. You can either take these dry or knock them down with a cold seltzer or prune juice. As a result, you may have a bit more gas coming through the back end that could signify the first rumblings of a bowel movement—now we're cooking with fire!

Don't Trust Anyone Who Doesn't Drink Coffee

OJM coffee variations include: a single/double espresso shot with a bissel of cream, an Americano with a splash of cream, or a drip coffee with a drop of cream. These measurements are precise and shouldn't disturb even the most lactose-intolerant Old Jewish Man.

Whether it's one hundred degrees in Los Angeles, Miami, Tel Aviv, or New York, do not, under any circumstances, drink iced coffee. Why? Because you're not a twenty-two-year-old youth saddled with debt interning at Pinterest. It doesn't take a genius to know that a plastic cup filled to the brim with ice cubes is where they get you. As soon as they add ice, the drink price rockets from three dollars to five. Wake up, sheeple!

Walking and the Light Jog

Take the first stroll of the day in whatever shoes are directly next to the door. Old Jewish Men of Florida, for instance, look no further than loose slippers or flip-flops. Be efficient in your daily routine. Your best bet is a pair of loose-fitting Velcro New Balances. These are comfortable sneakers with good support that can be used for either strolling or a light jog. A stroll can be taken every day, but a light jog—equal to the distance of two New York City blocks—shouldn't exceed three times per week. Less is always more.

Spread Etiquette

The breakfast spread is a sacred time that's just a mistake away from being completely wrong. Don't rush it, and don't let anyone rush you. Be prepared to ask questions such as: "Is this real cream or some fake soy crap?" "What putz got the low-fiber granola?" "This is toasted! I wanted my bagel *un*toasted! How am I supposed to eat this?"

Over the course of the spread, the newspaper will commute several times between table and bathroom, but it makes little difference to an Old Jewish Man where he reads the box scores. Think of the toilet as a second breakfast table. A home away from home, if you will. (Note: The Torah orders that no food is allowed in the facilities.) Some fellas require extreme solitude during this time, while others have been known to take important calls on the can. This is why going to the latrine is called "taking a meeting." Business-minded fellas require several newspapers or a few magazines to stay current on gold futures, obits, and currency markets. It's also perfectly acceptable to call up defense attorneys, cardiologists, dentists, or the rabbi. This is your time—take as long as you need.

> "To smoke and have coffee—and if you do it together, it's fantastic."
>
> —*Peter Falk*, **Wings of Desire**

Death Shouldn't Get in the Way of Resentment

After the spread, you will retire to the den to make calls for an hour before falling asleep. These aren't just friendly catch-ups but rather important follow-ups. It's essential to keep a running tab on which friends are alive, dying, or dead. Without this information, it's difficult to know who to invite for golf tomorrow. If you hear of a friend's passing, you should call their family to make sure that they're definitely gone and not just trying to extract pity from you. It's only after a close friend has kicked the bucket that you can start to say nice things about them. But remember, just because someone is dead doesn't mean you should stop resenting them. Holding a deep grudge is a key life-extender.

Video Chattin'

When it comes to technology, you will be expected to know how to tell someone else to open a Zoom link or answer a FaceTime call for you. For the fellas who had it all figured out in 2020, Covid was the perfect excuse to see people only on the golf course, where it was safe to swing from a healthy distance. Back home in the den, Old Jewish Men love Zooming in and out of boring events like so-and-so's wedding, some long-lost nephew's kid's bris, Melvin Schneer's grandson's bar mitzvah, and whatever else doesn't require a nine iron and a hot dog. If only there was a way to Zoom away from your wife when she asks you what you think about her new outfit.

FUTZING AROUND THE GREEN

"Golf is the only sport where you can practice every day for six months and not get any better."

—Larry David

DESPITE YOUR AGE, you should commit to maintaining a vicious competitive spirit until your very last breath. Hang on with an iron grip to the life-preserving spite, pettiness, and vindictiveness that has powered you from birth to old age. And there's no better place to employ these essential, rejuvenating character traits than on the green. Only here on the golf course can an Old Jewish Man spend a lovely, sunny afternoon doing everything in his power to defeat and humiliate his opponents. Fore!

Cheating: It's What the Other Guy Does

You will rarely find an Old Jewish Man who does not, after every shank on the fairway, baselessly accuse another OJM of cheating. *"I saw you free-dropping near the sand trap, Bob!"* Crafting believable cheating allegations and sticking to them until death is almost more important than winning the game itself. This advanced golf tactic (i.e., destroying the reputation of the friend you've known since archery class at Camp Boiberik in 1957) requires years of carefully crafted character debasement. You will need to plant these seeds early in your relationships and cultivate them for decades like a master bonsai artist. Play fair.

Never Concede

Under no circumstance should you admit that another fella is better than you. Take it to the grave. They should die thinking that their chip shot can't compete with yours. It doesn't matter how much you like them or how clearly superior they are at the game—never acknowledge it. In life there is your point of view, some other schmuck's point of view, and the truth.

Golf Is for Closers

Where else but on the fairway can an Old Jewish Man get five solid hours with a potential business partner? In addition to their masochistic love of the game and a peerless desire to subjugate one's so-called friends, OJM know that the golf course is the perfect place to SFB (Schmooze For Business). If an OJM suffers the unfortunate luck of pursuing his business mark in the company of regular golf companions, thwart off any threat of looking like a bum by degrading your pals tout suite. This is the time to puff out that barrel chest and channel those Mossad programs you've watched on the History Channel. Get in their head.

The MJ–OJM Connection

Cigars: check. Penchant for gambling: check. Shirts and pants four sizes too big: check. No, we aren't talking about your cousin Leo or Uncle Shnitz. We mean MJ. His Airness. The greatest ballplayer who ever lived. That's right, Michael Jordan. The GOAT is such a natural OJM that he could teach the younger class a thing or two about how to dress on the golf course. Jordan is cranky, bald, spiteful, highly competitive, perpetually drenched in sweat, loves to make a fuss, dresses like he's lived in Boca West the last thirty years, and would maybe run over his own mother to get a better score on the green. Sound familiar?

Always Have a Joke

Your job is to grind down opponents day after day on the green with terrible play and an arsenal of at least ten jokes that everyone has heard dozens of times. It's a long, grueling game, so keep plenty of stories in the stockpile too. You know the sort: anecdotes that make you seem far more important, rich, savvy, and universally adored than you are. If, however, you want fellas to keep calling you up to play, you better replenish your material every once in a while and occasionally make fun of yourself without encouraging them. In addition to your joke arsenal and a stash of good cigars, never let a guy buy you a hot dog two outings in a row. Also, make friends with all the employees at the country club—they decide who gets the good tee times. Every staff member gets a bottle of cognac or Scotch on Christmas. Sure, gift-giving for gentile holidays is painful, but if it gets you on the green, it's great value. Think of it as an investment.

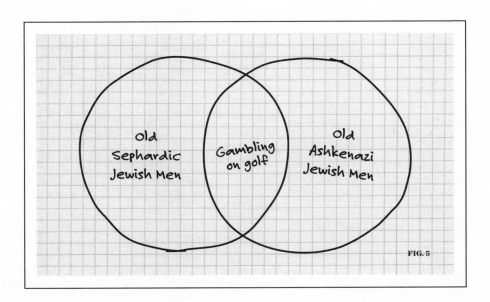

Old Sephardic Jewish Men

Gambling on golf

Old Ashkenazi Jewish Men

FIG. 5

Gone Shvitzing

If the club doesn't have a shvitz, don't go. Doesn't matter who else golfs there, or what Protestant somebody told some Catholic nobody that this is the top place to knock eighteen holes—no shvitz, no golf. A locker room needs a few basics if a club wants Old Jewish Men to shell out for a membership: bottomless towels, quality toilet paper, body cream, and a functioning shvitz that should be kept running at a minimum four thousand degrees.

You won't require fancy scents in the air or cucumber mint water—you just need a hot, sweaty room where you can be naked in peace. Young pishers seem to think that the shvitz is like a monastery to be quiet and think. That may be so when you're some big shot or intellectual type, but for OJM, it's simply a place to hang out with the fellas. Being naked with friends is what life is all about.

One towel is never good enough. Take two (at least).

"The only thing more powerful than inflation is an unabashedly naked old guy in the locker room."

—*Jerome Powell,* possibly

The Finishing Touch: Leisure Suits

After futzing through eighteen holes and a shvitz, it's time to shower, towel off, and get dressed. Don't just throw on any old piece of crap—that's for classless youngsters. No, no, when you've just spent the last two hours sweating out nothing but nitrates, cigar stink, and relish, you need comfortable clothing that makes a fella feel like he's taken care of, while also maintaining the sensation of being completely naked. That's where the leisure suit comes in. The entire point of this magical garment is to match the luxuriant sensation a fella has in the shvitz as he sits there in nothing but a cup of his own sweat. Pro tip: Cotton beats polyester every time.

Congrats—you're now well on your way to living forever.

WHAT TO BRING TO THE SHVITZ

1. AM radio

2. Several newspapers

3. Tax forms; accounting documents; will

4. Cold seltzer

5. Candy (or anything to keep the blood sugar up)

6. Athlete's foot cream

7. Toenail clippers

8. Lotion/Vaseline

9. Sweat rag

10. Personal thermometer (to make sure it's hot enough!)

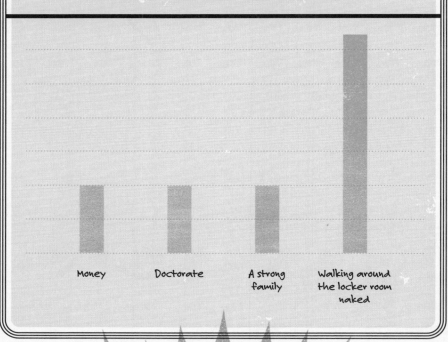

THINGS THAT GIVE OLD JEWISH MEN A SENSE OF POWER

Money

Doctorate

A strong family

Walking around the locker room naked

"The main thing you gotta be is naked. No one cares how much you're packing as long as you're proud. Not to say that some guys aren't impressive—good for them."

Joey Bieberman, 88, retired stock trader, on OJM steam room etiquette

THE OLD JEWISH MEN'S GUIDE

THE LEGEND OF WAYNE DIAMOND, AN OJM IMMORTAL

Wayne Diamond is a lot of things, but a typical-looking guy isn't one of them. The man sticks out like a whack-a-mole, and that's the way he wants it. The next time you see him cracking pepper over his gnocchi at Elio's, go up and talk to him—he won't mind. The truth is this Diamond guy is a major success. He may look like he owns casinos in Reno or a large stake in a tanning oil wholesaling business, but Wayne made his dough the old fashioned way: in the schmatta biz. These days you can catch him on the silver screen, which explains the seizure-warning bright ivories in his mouth.

Wayne's the embodiment of the saying, "You can't buy taste," which makes everything about him that much more entertaining. He spends most days in his underwear live streaming himself tossing spaghetti, ranting about the ruin of modern man. Wayne stays mostly in Wayne's World, a deeply tanned Floridian hyper-chamber of vino, pasta, and sun baths where the only mission is to be, in his own words, "like, *really* Wayne Diamond now." Sign me up, Daddy-O.

WAYNE'S NOTABLE QUOTES:

- "When you're a gambler, losing is the biggest part of it. Once you lose, you gotta win it back."

- "People look like slobs."

- "Chino pants should be outlawed in every restaurant in New York. Striped shirts and checked shirts: They should throw you out of a restaurant."

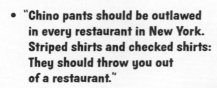

Possibly Gentile

This breed of oddly kind Old Jewish Men knows how to work a grill, can get through an entire meal without yelling to prove their point, and feels no need to self-deprecate. Possibly Gentile fellas are not only capable of listening when someone else is talking but in fact enjoy doing so. They have a knack for remembering names, dates, and events that have nothing to do with them and possess an honest fear of confrontation and social abrasion, which happens rarely anyway.

Possibly Gentiles often stand higher than five foot nine inches and have lustrous, thick white hair that covers their entire scalp (not just the sides). When the bowl clogs, they don't call a plumber; they understand the inner, deeper workings of the toilet beyond just the handle. These fellas rewind VHS tapes, grasp the difference between a flathead and a Phillips, eat English muffins, own multiple ladders in different sizes, and know what a Tuff Shed is; they take apart and reassemble objects for the hell of it, use separate knives for peanut butter and jelly, aren't afraid of precipitation, and genuinely look forward to hosting friendly gatherings.

> "More mayo, anyone?"
>
> —CORINTHIANS 4:22

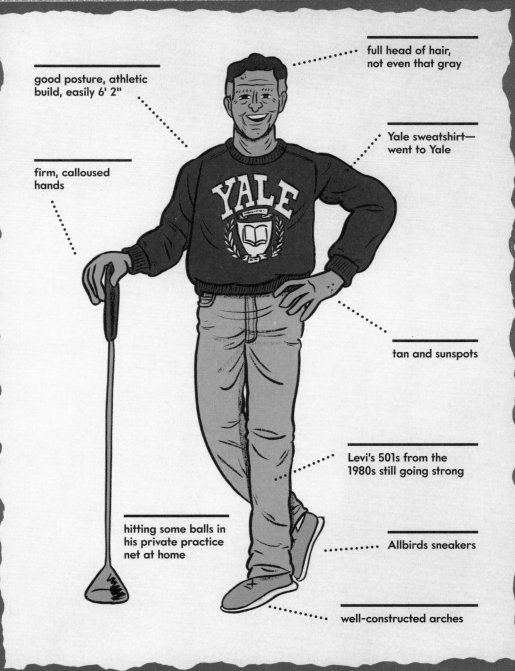

good posture, athletic build, easily 6' 2"

firm, calloused hands

full head of hair, not even that gray

Yale sweatshirt— went to Yale

tan and sunspots

Levi's 501s from the 1980s still going strong

hitting some balls in his private practice net at home

Allbirds sneakers

well-constructed arches

YALE

Suspiciously Thankful

On Shabbos, Possibly Gentile OJM wear those weird white-cotton yarmulkes they give away at shul. They can hardly read Hebrew, own only transliterated prayer books, and actually *observe* Thanksgiving instead of eating as much and as fast as they can until they're sick. These guys insist Turkey Day is a fantastic opportunity to "show humility" and gratitude for our founding fathers, and they like to remind everyone at the table "breaking bread" with them (yes, they call it "breaking bread") that America has always been a decent place for the Jewish people, even if it's getting harder and harder to find a good bialy.

Boozing Like a Gentile

When Possibly Gentile OJM come home from a long, fulfilling day in periodontology, accounting, ophthalmology, or philanthropy, they unwind with alcohol instead of eating themselves into a coma. They like to mention how their physicians encourage them to "take a load off" with a cocktail and that it's merely a "relaxant." Drinking liquor is a point of pride for these fellas, and it's almost like they're rubbing it in the faces of other Old Jewish Men at weddings and bar mitzvahs that their svelte bodies can handle the abuse.

If you ask them a question about their health, Possibly Gentiles (who tend to be incredibly weight-conscious and exercise constantly) will happily pontificate about the difference between LDL and HDL cholesterol and can articulate the dangers of trans fat. At least someone knows what that stuff is.

Getting Honest with the Man Upstairs

When you see them at shul, they look out of place in their popped collars, towering over the congregation with perfect posture, and they're almost always chosen for hagbah. Possibly Gentile OJM have an earnest, unpolluted relationship with religion that other breeds of OJM find off-putting, even horrifying. These fellas love to raise an emphatic hand high in the air at the Shabbos dinner table or at synagogue to ask the rabbi a heartfelt or overly academic question. They often wonder if they're doing something right or following the rules, and they love to say things like, "G-d is everywhere, all around us, all the time." Hopefully not through Hal Finger's wedding speech. What a yawn.

It's no surprise that Possibly Gentiles have trouble making friends with other OJM types and usually stick to themselves. You'll notice these fellas move in packs and have their own poker games. Good luck finding them gambling with the other OJM. For these guys, poker is a methodical, mathematical game instead of a quick way to eat a lot of food, complain about the wife, crack jokes, and lose your house title. Pick your poison.

OBIT by J.G. WINTHROP, *Kennebunkport Gazette*

POSSIBLY GENTILE, WHO AMASSED

what is widely considered the world's foremost collection of ancient Italian wide-wale corduroy and donated it to the Metropolitan Museum of Art, along with enough money to build a new wing called Assimilation Hall, died at his home on the Upper East Side of Manhattan on Sunday, his favored day of rest. The cause was cardiac arrest, said his son. At the time, Mr. Gentile was refereeing a game of croquet that became suddenly unpleasant.

"All my life is passing in front of my eyes.
The worst part of it is I'm driving a used car."

—*Some Old Jewish Man* at 7th Avenue Donuts

CHAPTER 5

Gettin' Around

No one knows the city, town, or gated subdivision better than you. This is why you should *never* ask for directions. It doesn't matter how lost you get or how desperate you are for a brisket sandwich, insulin needle, or toilet—DNAFD. DO. NOT. ASK. FOR. DIRECTIONS.

But beyond maintaining a talmudic knowledge of the city grid, transportation options abound, and as an OJM, it's your job to have an opinion on every single one of them.

The Original MapQuest

The only people who know better than a map are Old Jewish Men, and nothing should make you happier than directing a group of lost Iowans to a Broadway show. Be sure to tell them twelve different ways to get from West 23rd Street to West 57th without taking a cab. Remember, directions are for bumbling tourists, out-of-town know-nothings, should-move-back-to-the-burbs interlopers, and unemployable morons. No self-respecting OJM asks for help when he can walk around in circles for hours. That's what life's all about.

So how best to get from Point A to Point B? Let's break it down.

Shufflin' Along

WASN'T IT MAIMONIDES who said that the best part of life is walking around looking at things and quietly judging people? Sounds like him. At any rate, the truth is that trudging the block in your Velcro speedsters armed with nothing but a scowl is the best show in town, and there's no price of admission!

Master Shufflers know the city like the back of this morning's knish. There's an equation for everything and efficiency is key: Strides to the grocery store, the shrink, the corner diner, your bookie's apartment, and the podiatrist's office are all expert calculations. When another neighborhood shuffler (i.e. an associate) mentions that they just hired a new girl at the cheese shop down the block—now that's your kind of party—you'll already know it's exactly 242 shuffles away. This is your territory, and if for some reason you're invited somewhere outside the shuffling radius, a firm "Are you out of your mind?" usually does the trick.

Ridin' the Rails

SOMETIMES THE SUBWAY is a little late or crowded, but it will take you wherever you need to go on a nicely discounted senior fare. Being master of your domain means knowing every train route in the city and happily dropping dead rather than consulting a subway map.

A few words of advice: Never sit in a middle seat and don't touch anything. If someone tries to talk to you, growl. If they try to touch you, mace 'em. Even if a cute young woman and her infant need directions, ignore 'em—questions should be asked on the platform. Once you're inside the train car itself you're an animal. It's every man for himself. Only the strong survive. Eh, fine, lady. Where do you need to go? Take the 3 to Times Square and get on the Q for two stops.

Coming and Going

There's fifty ways to get from Coney Island to Midtown, then over to the Upper East Side and back down to Kew Gardens, and they're all best enjoyed with a hot cup of joe and a newspaper. No bagel, no cream cheese, no food on the train. People who eat on trains are disgusting and should be shunned. A coffee must be strongly lidded and hotter than Gene Tierney.

Now that you've read the paper and caught up on the price of crude oil, you're on your way. If you happen to be French, the commute from Notre Dame to Belleville for Chinese food is best enjoyed with the pages of *Le Monde*. After all, you gotta be on top of *le président*'s latest sexual conquests. If there are no seats available on your train, groan and grab your back until somebody offers you one. Don't say *merci*, either. It's your right.

"I would rather drive around aimlessly for a half hour than ask some stranger for directions."

—*Saul S. Sunkman*, 102, retired dentist, Berkshires resident

Sailin' the Seas

YOU SHOULD KNOW exactly how much the Staten Island Ferry costs (that's a trick—it's free), when it leaves, when it was built, and how long to the millisecond it takes to get from St. George to the Whitehall Terminal in Manhattan—not to mention how the hours of operation, seats, and bathrooms have changed year over year for the last four decades. Not only are you expected to maintain a bottomless supply of ready-to-go complaints about the new ferry route, snack options, and rude ticket punchers, but you should also keep a laundry list of reasons why alternative transport is superior to the garden variety. Why waste gas when there are ferries, streetcars, trolleys, rickshaws, cable cars, trams, and trolley buses?

Despite your jabbering, the truth is you haven't taken the Staten Island Ferry in forty years and have only seen pictures of streetcars and trollies from Denver and San Francisco—but you've watched *Vertigo* seventy-six times. That's right—you're an expert.

Cruisin' in the Whip

LONGTIME NEW YORK CITY public official and OJM Hall of Famer Robert Moses, who is now widely maligned after Robert Caro's book *The Power Broker* revealed him to be an egotistical, power-hungry maniac, spent his entire career making the Big Apple more car-centric. But Moses himself neither owned an automobile nor knew how to drive one. This is a classic OJM move.

A love of cars does not necessarily mean a love of driving. It's hard on the nerves, tough on the eyes, and the pedals can be strenuous for weak ankles. If you do own a car, make sure to let it sit in the garage year after year because you either have no idea how to operate it or prefer to take the train anyway. No matter how expensive the insurance and storage fees are, don't get rid of your wheels—you never know when you might need to escape another pogrom.

You should, however, know how to talk about cars. Spend time leering at them and admiring their paint jobs, wiring, and overall sleekness. And always have a trusted mechanic who won't rip you off since you have no clue how these machines actually work. But that doesn't mean you haven't studied the history of the automobile and can recite pointless facts at the drop of a hat about discontinued antique models or the Italian sports car that some Fellini character drove.

Gentile Magic

When gentile men so much as touch cars, they can't help but make them better. Their hands seem to possess magical mechanical powers, while Old Jewish Men's hands are utterly useless, as if solely designed to turn the pages of the Talmud and damage fine machinery. Is it any wonder that you see sports cars coming out of Bavaria and Bologna, but not Fort Lauderdale? In minutes, a gentile is tightening the cupholder with a handy pocket screwdriver, testing the brakes with a steady foot, and recommending oil changes, while an OJM leans over him, nodding, contributing nothing but body heat. "That piece looks broken," he may tell the gentile. "You should fix it."

Coffee-stained leather seats

Hairpiece flying in the wind

Car won in poker game

Tires haven't been rotated since Eisenhower

What's in the Garage

Having several cars means you can move them from one side of the street to the other, from the back of the garage to the front of the driveway, or into a friend's garage (which can take an entire day). This may all seem like an imposition, but killing time with cars is precisely the point. Simply watching someone you hired repaint, refinish, retread, untread, de-tread, weatherproof, oil, cool, and heat your vehicle can take hours.

Cars are an endless time suck, which means an OJM can spend entire days in the garage futzing around without accomplishing a thing. Now that's heaven!

Hoppin' on the Bike

I T'S BEEN SAID THAT Einstein thought up the theory of relativity while futzing around on a bike—and if pedaling was good enough for Al, it's good enough for you. So forget subways and cars for a second and consider the humble, trusty bike. Yes, bicycles require the expenditure of energy, but you never have to worry about parking—a power-sapping nightmare in its own right. And for all you geniuses keeping score, biking is faster than walking (easier on the knees too). Plus, there's always a pole or a gate to lean the bike on at the Food Coop. It's the only free thing you'll ever find in Park Slope.

slightly more expensive bike than riding partner's

Prescription sunglasses

Zero leg hair

Pedal Weather

If an Old Jewish Man doesn't have to break a sweat and the outside conditions are ideal for pedaling (clear skies, no traffic), then one of these fellas will happily use a bike to get to where he needs to go. This is what's called Pedal Weather. This is an important term. Write that down.

Hills Are a Nonstarter

There should be nothing remotely athletic or strenuous about a bike trip. Lose the spandex, and forget click-in shoes, neon orange sunglasses, crotch cups, and on-shirt water bottle holders. This isn't exercise, it's uncomplicated transportation that should lessen the wear and tear on certain joints. If there's a hill, you can forget it. An Old Jewish Man won't even ride his bike downhill, as he knows perfectly well that eventually he'll have to climb back up it. Hills are like favors—don't ask for one if you know you'll have to return it.

Flyin' the Friendly Skies

IT'S TIME TO START thinking ahead. Weeks or even months before any trip—either domestic or overseas—an OJM must prepare himself for the excursion. To prepare for airplane travel, you gotta pack for all weather conditions because you're not buying a crappy parka in an overpriced store in a tourist-trap Spanish town. Packing is like lying on your taxes—it's gotta be done the right way. That means the correct shoes with tread and arch support, a variety of socks with different thicknesses, weatherproof pants, a protective hat, and plenty of sunscreen, bug spray, and sweat-resistant underwear.

OJM Airplane Starter Pack

Schmooze the Desk Jockey

It's time to haggle for a better seat on the plane. It doesn't matter how old you are, how much dough you have in the bank, or what you've accomplished in life—an OJM never shells out for premium legroom. You will refuse to be gouged by greedy airlines on principle alone. It's better to be cramped and righteous than comfortable and ripped off.

Here's an essential maneuver you must perform immediately upon entering the airport terminal: Convince whatever miserable face is pecking away behind the airline desk that you are too feeble, too incontinent, or too *anything* to sit in either (1) the middle seat or (2) the back of the plane. Do whatever it takes to convince that underpaid, overworked gate agent to give you (1) an aisle seat that is (2) near the front. And if they still refuse, strongly suggest—shout, if you must—that you may be stinking up the entire two-hundred–person plane with your (1) urinary tract infection, (2) benign prostatic hyperplasia, or (3) incontinence. Repeat the words *colostomy bag* several times. Mention that, due to tight hips, bad feet, and old-man circulation, it is medically recommended that you not sit in the cheap seats.

It makes little difference whether any of this is true—there's a good chance anyway that, on one of your many trips to the lavatory, the slightest bit of turbulence will send you flying through the aisles.

Choppin' It Up

DOTTING AROUND THE New York, Paris, or Miami skyline in a bird means you've got a busy day with a lot of decisions to make and a scrum of annoying people asking you for things. "Sign this, sign that"; "Pay this, pay that"; "More cream, another Danish?"

For a high-powered Business OJM (see next page) with a chopper, the irritating sound of honking horns from congested roadways below becomes more theoretical with every rip through the sky. Michael Bloomberg has been known to fly his helicopter through all weather conditions and enjoys the reputation of being a fine host to his passengers. Those who have traveled on Bloomberg's chopper remember him offering complimentary coffee and cream from a thermos, and he even asked if anyone was nauseated— although that probably had a little something to do with not wanting to soil the leather.

Making Good Time

Nelson Peltz, a crotchety New York OJM who made his fortune in the frozen food business, pissed off more than a few neighbors when he started commuting forty miles into Manhattan by chopper from his mansion in Bedford, New York. While everyone on the ground was stewing in traffic, Peltz was up there in the sky playing solitaire, slurping macchiatos in the cockpit, and making great time. If you ever stake your fortune and become an untouchable OJM Businessman, you gotta master the art of being reviled in style. These fellas have more simultaneous lawsuits filed against them than teeth in their mouth, but once you get up to cruising altitude, the plebeian voices have a way of diminishing. And if they don't, turn off your hearing aid.

Business Jews
aka The Billionaire Club

These are the big shots. Forget being a millionaire, Business OJM throw away fifty mil running for president out of spite. Their wives get off on the lifestyle while they get off on the game. They're usually self-made, grew up hard in Brooklyn, fought in wars, and then lucked into inventing idiotically lucrative things like sugar packets, screw tops, and the nozzle.

From deep Brooklyn to Star Island to Monaco to Switzerland, Business OJM can sniff out opportunity in a puddle of subway puke. They've spent their lives barely sleeping—every second exists to make more deals. These fellas are closers who don't need to yell to get things done and possess one key character trait that keeps them at the top of their game: They don't see the world in terms of huge swings and paradigm shifts. Everything returns to equilibrium, and disasters won't send them running for the hills. Nah, Business OJM make small, meaningful adjustments and move operations to Palm Beach bubbles, multi-apartment Upper East Side sprawls, Westchester ranches, Telluride mansions, and recently acquired pieds-à-terre on Cadogan Square. They spend their free time playing chess, inhaling *The Economist*, and throwing away hundreds of millions on dinosaur bones and French castles they'll never visit. They drink sherry, study financial charts, and have reread *The Passage of Power*.

definitely identifies as Republican but hates Trump

tidy hair, well groomed

Freemason pin

bespoke Oxford suit, super 160s merino

still subscribes to *The Economist*

"In God we trust. All others must bring data."

bridal leather briefcase flapping open

ancient tassel loafers shined by his guy on 51st Street

Wake Me Up at 50,000 Deaths

Business OJM can spend weeks alone in huge, paneled home offices whipping through hundreds of pages of documents. Nothing gets them revved up like debt restructuring. When asked about a new philanthropic project or recent acquisition, this breed will most likely say something like "I couldn't be more excited," while their face betrays an incurable inner pain, a tragic death in the family, or inveterate boredom. When things go off the rails in the world—terrorism, disease, stock market crashes—these fellas go on CNBC to make bland, noncommittal statements that put the rest of us at ease. Without their predictable, emotionless rambling, we may have to count on ourselves for information and comfort—and that would be a disaster.

BUSINESS OJM READING LIST

The Power Broker, Robert Caro

Mastering the Market Cycle, Howard Marks

John Quincy Adams: Militant Spirit, James Traub

The Brothers Karamazov, Fyodor Dostoevsky

Poland: The First Thousand Years, Patrice M. Dabrowski

Don't Argue with Facts

At social gatherings, Business OJM can be found with a drink in their hand, saying something like "In business, if you want a friend, get a dog." Are they happy? Of course not. They live to predict inverted bond yields or Colombian drought cycles, which is even less fun than it sounds.

These fellas might read as stiff or withholding, but in fact they want you to succeed. After all, this is how efficient markets work. Productivity is key, immigration essential. A buck is a buck, a deal is a deal, and Business OJM think of themselves as part of the great American experiment. Remember, they came from nothing and don't mind taking the subway. They tip fairly but not extravagantly and get regular colonoscopies. When you spend your life closing deals, printing bucks, buying property, and building nothing into something, you wanna keep going until the very end. Lots of gas and no brakes. The action is the juice.

OBIT by GARVIN A. GOLD, *Wall Street Journal*

MR. BUSINESS OJM IS SURVIVED

by his wife, two siblings, four children, ten grandchildren, and twenty-one great-grandchildren — all of whom are at his duplex apartment right now, glaring at each other under the Rothkos, dealmaking about who gets the silver, quietly flirting with the lawyer who was appointed executor, claiming their toddlers have a special fondness for grandpa's Giacomettis, slipping World War II medals and medallions awarded by the French government into their blazer pockets, and whispering bitterly to their mothers about how Susannah's fiancé shouldn't be given a cent until they're married.

CHAPTER 6

The Art of the Schmooze

Most Old Jewish Men want for nothing and couldn't care less about working the room—which is exactly why they're so damn good at it. Having zero desire happens to be the number-one most advantageous trait for schmoozers in the field. It is the epitome of natural talent. It's like being a basketball player with wings. And while your average OJM schmoozer is merely food- and leisure-focused, there's another breed of more refined and calculating OJM who's playing the long game.

The schmooze is built on chitchat. Some have spent decades refining their craft to needle and seduce and win over producers, actors, doctors, lawyers, bank tellers, waiters, towel boys, over-the-counter customers, secretaries, politicians, and corporate lackeys into getting exactly what they want. There are casual OJM schmoozers who charm and woo for an extra side of home fries, and then there are the big-time players who can talk entire companies into selling at an outrageous share price.

Of course, schmoozing in and of itself isn't conniving or calculated (not that there's anything wrong with that!). Many OJM schmooze innocently, chatting with no ulterior motive, while others will think only of the endgame.

After carefully studying the OJM at right, you'll come to understand that schmoozers come in all different styles. Turn the page for a not-very-short anecdote about Sauly Bernstein, a Brooklyn-born OJM turned famed Los Angeles comedy writer who thirty years later was given a second life . . . all thanks to the art of the schmooze. Remember, some fellas are naturals, while others spend a lifetime learning this ancient art form. What sort of schmoozer are you?

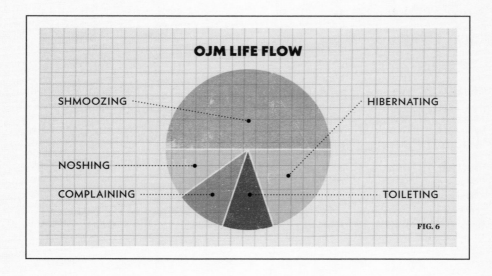

OJM LIFE FLOW

SHMOOZING

HIBERNATING

NOSHING

COMPLAINING

TOILETING

FIG. 6

SOME IDENTIFIABLE SCHMOOZING STYLES

THE AGGRESSIVELY SOCIAL FAST-TALKERS: Known for their wild hand movements and selling over-market Brooklyn real estate.

THE UNDERCOVER FELLAS WITH AN AGENDA: Live on golf courses in South Florida and Los Angeles and will do just about anything, including giving holiday gifts, to keep their memberships. (See story on page 138.)

THE NON-AGENDA-AGENDA SLOW PLAYERS: Can take years to befriend you and will invite you to dinner for decades, waiting for you to sell your parking lot so they can swoop in at a good price. They'll die waiting.

THE HEART-TO-HEART FAMILIARITY MANIPULATORS: Tend to be Possibly Gentile (see page 116) and will use emotional depth to draw you in. How do you gain trust? By giving it.

THE "I'VE SEEN IT ALL AND NEED NOTHIN' FROM YA" HIGH ROLLERS: Live on caviar and vodka in the towers of Midtown Manhattan and live to keep winning. They always know the price of a gallon of milk.

THE MASTERS-OF-WIT JOKE-ACCELERATION VIRTUOSOS: Always ready with a wisecrack. You'll find these men glad-handing in delis all over Los Angeles. Once they know you like them, they'll try to get on your show.

THE CHARMING BUT CLUELESS SAVANTS: You may think they're oblivious, but these guys want something. Maybe it's nothing more than the last few bites of your tuna sandwich, but either way . . .

THE BACK-SLAPPING, GREGARIOUS-BUT-SELF-HATING UNDERDOGS: Don't be fooled by their self-deprecation, these OJM know the pity game well and will prey on a kind heart. Give them a little taste, and they'll take you for the full monty. Visit them in the hospital once, and the next thing you know they're moving into your bungalow, eating all your food, and guffawing with your wife.

THE WINNER-TAKE-ALL MACHERS: James Caan-esque fellas you might meet at Chicago pool halls. These guys don't mess around. They're rare, but they exist. The schmooze isn't always a humorous slow play.

"The Undercover Fella with an Agenda"

A Los Angeles Schmoozing Story, Starring Saul "Sauly" Bernstein

YOUR NAME IS SAULY Bernstein and today is your eighty-fifth birthday. You asked them not to surprise you because nothing gets you going anymore, except maybe a clean bill of health. But here you are at Factor's Deli celebrating another spin around the sun. You've reached the age when people are impressed simply by the fact you still exist.

"Do you have everything you need, Dad?" Olivia, your daughter, asks.

Everything but a twenty-one-year-old and a new prostate, you think.

"Sure, sure. I'm paying," you announce to the group. "Order anything else you want."

There are blintzes on the table—you haven't had one since you almost dropped dead more than thirty years ago. Your second wife, Elaine, is on her cell phone taking pictures of every single second that goes by.

"Give your wrist a rest," you tell her. "It's not like you're on the clock."

You were born in Sheepshead Bay but have spent the last fifty-five years in Los Angeles working as a TV writer. You got your big break in the 1990s through a magnificent act of schmoozing. It had been a desperate time. You'd written for *Taxi* and *All in the Family*, but success

couldn't have gotten through writing three seasons of *Taxi* without seltzer and peanuts. He liked that. "You're a comedy writer?" he asked.

You spent the night chatting about psychiatry and sibling rivalry, which you'd studied up on to impress him. He was a soft-spoken guy but argued like a yid. You said sibling rivalry has nothing to do with the siblings themselves, it's about impressing the mother. He'd never heard that before, so you asked if he wanted to hear the real story on Sigmund Freud. "It takes a while," you said, "but it gets to the motherfucking point." Curtis laughed, and the job was yours.

◇◇◇◇◇

"We have a big surprise for you, Dad," Olivia says.

"Okay," you say, browning coffee with creamer and slurping. You love the first sip of joe more than you love most people. The years go fast. These days, you get up from the toilet and another decade is in the can.

"Look, Sauly!" Elaine calls out. "They're putting you up on the wall!"

The owners of Factor's hover over your table. Olivia is next to them with her husband, a small-toothed, heavily mustached attorney, holding up a picture of you from your short-lived days as a stand-up, back when you

was cut short by your first coronary. When they let you out of the hospital, you struggled to get back in the game. You spent days cold-calling, digging for opportunities. Finally, you needled your old secretary to tell you about a showrunner named David Curtis who was pitching a spin-off around town about two psychiatrist brothers. You needed work. You were in debt—alimony isn't cheap.

So you dug up an old *TV Guide* interview where Curtis mentioned that he couldn't think straight without eating unshelled peanuts. You got the name of the bar in Santa Monica where he drank, plopped down on a stool with a two-pound bag of goobers, and de-shelled. When Curtis noticed, you joked that you had hair. It's going up right next to Jackie Mason.

"What a schmuck he was," you say. "But no one was funnier."

As you watch them hammer your picture into the wall, you can't help but hate Jackie even more than you did when he was alive.

"So? What do you think?" the owner wants to know.

"Why can't they hang me next to Raquel Welch?"

He laughs and asks how the pastrami tastes, eyeballing the uneaten sandwich on your table. "It has your name on it, Saul."

"I haven't had pastrami in thirty years. Doctor's orders."

"You only turn eighty-five once, Sauly." He's got a point.

As you bite into the hot pastrami a breathlessness washes over you. It's pathetic how much you missed the salty dripping meat. For years you've been obediently flumping dry turkey onto pale slices of grocery rye, buttering it with a teaspoon of mustard at your GP's request. As the cow fat liquifies around your lips, you smash your face deeper into the sandwich for an even greedier bite. Warm oil splashes, cooled by a nibble of pickle, and with it something else—a blurriness. The room spins and you're caught off guard by a familiar,

grating voice. *Sauly!* it squawks. *It's your mother, Sauly! Dinner!*

The room spins as you swim headlong into your childhood kitchen toward the burning food. Each step is heavier and heavier until your chest compacts into short, painful palpitations. It's a gut punch. You're airless. A sharp pang cuts into your core.

"You've suffered a coronary," a voice says flatly. You're in a hospital bed, and a man with dark, tired eyes inspects you with a flashlight.

"Another one?" you wheeze through a series of tubes.

"Relax your face, Saul."

The doctor explains that your latest heart attack is even more serious than the first. There's a roadblock in your artery that will require immediate lifestyle changes: no more salt— NONE—and light daily exercise to get the cholesterol down.

"Your blood hasn't circulated for years," the doctor says. "It's just been sitting there . . . clotting."

"What about surgery?" you heave.

"No. Cut salt. Play golf. Eat right."

You belong to a country club but haven't swung the sticks for a decade.

"What about surgery?" you repeat, rasping.

"Sauly, the block is deep in the left ventricle," he explains. "There's a small pump that needs to be replaced. Think of it like trying to find a tiny screw for a BMW that was made in 1972. How many screws like that are just laying around? And even if you find one, would anyone know how to put it in?"

What's life without salt? you wonder. There must be a quick fix. Isn't that the point of modern medicine?

"The best heart surgeon in the world lives in Los Angeles," the doctor continues. "He did Rodney Dangerfield's aorta, but he's impossible to get. You'll be dead three decades before he sees you."

"Jewish guy?"

"No, not this one. It's Dr. William Frederick Rudolph."

You recognize the name. He's . . . a golfer. You belong to the same club.

"I've seen him around."

"I hear he's harder than a coffin nail," says the doctor. "You're gonna have to schmooze."

Two months later you're in your '92 Beemer with the top down, cruising Olympic Boulevard potholes, golf clubs jingling in the back. The only Old Jewish Men who refuse to drive German cars are the ones who can't afford them.

Lately you've been living on nothing but rice crackers, spinach, and Activia. Things are getting dire. For the last twenty years, aside from the occasional medically induced sexual excursion, eating is life's only thrill.

You roll up to the club and the kid there helps you with your golf bag. You pass through the locker room, glad-handing fellas you recognize. Jack Hartman just finished shooting eighteen and sips mint water with some reptilian-looking specimen who calls himself a film producer. Everyone's a producer, but of what?

"Does Rudolph still come around?" you ask Jack.

"The doc? Yeah, Rudolph did my surgery years ago," he says. He lifts up his shirt, showing off the scar in the center of his chest.

"How'd you score that?" you ask.

"We've been playing in the same card game twenty years. I got in before Rudolph was a big shot. Now he chooses his patients—no one knows how or why. Luckily, my ticker still runs like an Italian espresso machine—it'll be years before I need new gaskets. I can eat salt right out of the shaker."

"Can you put a word in for me?"

"It's not the DMV, Sauly. Rudolph and Rudolph alone decides who lives and who dies."

You spend the next couple weeks canvassing the golf club, trying to corner the elusive doctor. You see him alone by the drinking fountain, catching heat in the sauna, eating grilled cheese at a table for one in the club, but can't find the right moment to approach. It's like talking to a pretty girl at a mixer. One day, a week later, you're in the clubhouse suffering through another cold salad when Rudolph sits down nearby. He orders a cheeseburger with muenster and a glass of Edelweiss and opens a newspaper.

"Hey, great-looking lunch! How'd my Marlins do last night?" you ask, trying to start a conversation.

Rudolph peers into your bowl of flavorless greens before steering back to the newspaper. This one doesn't schmooze easy.

That night you read up on Rudolph. There's not a lot there, but you notice a through line in his career: From Don Rickles's liver transplant to Jerry Lewis's open-heart surgery, he operates mostly on Jews—famous funny Jews.

"I'm extending not only life, but a world of laughter," Rudolph explains to the *Wall Street Journal* when asked about the titanium valve he installed in Rodney Dangerfield's left aorta. "Laughter is the pinnacle of human emotion." Hmm. You might've just found your Rosetta Stone.

One evening, a week later, your phone rings.

"Sauly, Jack Hartman from the club," the voice says. "I know it's short notice, but we need a sixth for stud. Gussy Shultz got a UTI from his catheter. Can you make it to Rudolph's place in Hancock Park in an hour?"

The next thing you know you're speeding down La Brea like a maniac. This is your chance to get close to the big guy. There's nothing like the camaraderie of gambling.

You whipsaw through a turn and park outside. The doctor's loaded. The house is huge and there are six German sports cars in the driveway, not including yours.

At the card table, Rudolph avoids eye contact. He hasn't acknowledged your presence outside of dealing you in. As he shuffles cards between his long, thin fingers, you wonder how deeply and thoroughly he could examine a ticker with those talons.

The buy-in isn't cheap, but you'd spend ten grand to sit here all night with Rudolph, waiting for your chance to schmooze. It's obvious that every one of the men at the game is determined to stay in the doctor's good graces—they could be just one pastrami triple-decker away from oblivion too. Jack alludes to his open-heart surgery several times while bragging about the leading ladies he schtupped in the seventies. Aside from Rudolph, everyone at the table laughs freely, gratuitously. *Laughter is currency*, you think.

The men around the table live carelessly. Since you've been off salt, you're more aware of the behavior. Another guy, Bobby Casablanca, is a hotheaded finger licker, a retired actor who pounds gourmet Gouda and keeps a bottle of Gaviscon next to his chip stack. Rudolph eats cheese slowly, butters each gourmet cracker, and sips cold gin. He's all logistics—betting, shuffling, mucking, and, slowly but surely, winning. You notice the other players fold big hands against him and each time offer up a similar ass-kissing comment: "Well played, Doctor." Between hands the jokes are for Rudolph's benefit. A table of dancing monkeys clamoring for approval from the good surgeon who has yet to crack a smile.

"Have you guys heard the one about the two Jews walking down the street?" Rudolph says meekly.

You look at the other fellas. The room draws silent. Chewing and smacking subsides as the men set their wide, pandering eyes on the doctor.

"Benny is walking down the road with his friend, Max, when he suddenly says, 'You know what, Max, I'm a walking economy.' 'Whatever do you mean by that?' asks Max. 'Well, it's like this: My hairline is in recession, my stomach is a victim of inflation, and the combination of these factors is putting me into a depression!'"

Everyone bursts out laughing like hyenas. You've heard bad jokes like this all your life. They're not worthy of a fart, let alone a laugh.

"That's an all-timer, doc," Casablanca says assembling another sandwich. "Great material."

Rudolph rattles off mediocre line after mediocre line, all met with painful fake enthusiasm. *What the hell is this?* you think. Rudolph's too smart not to know they're only laughing to get bumped up the waitlist. Have any of them succeeded in getting anything out of this guy? They're his chew toys, a groveling swarm of geriatric marionettes. It's infuriating. Forget schmoozing, the phoniness is a disgrace to comedy.

You interrupt—it's time to shoot your shot. "Are we playing poker or telling bad jokes?"

Everyone turns to you. The room is silent as Rudolph rotates a chip in his long fingers.

"Am I not entertaining you?" the doctor asks.

"Your jokes should come with a warning label," you say. "Your ass must be jealous with the amount of shit flying out of your mouth."

Rudolph sits silently and fidgets the chip some more, as if spectating.

"What have you ever done—you think you're so funny?" Casablanca shouts.

"I don't engage in mental combat with the unarmed," you bite back. "Or the ugly. It looks like your face caught on fire and someone tried to put it out with a nine iron."

The table laughs. Casablanca cowers. Rudolph looks as if he may crack.

"I wrote lines that won Emmys. I brought laughs to every home in America."

"Daytime Emmys," Casablanca mutters back.

"If I wanted to hear from an asshole, I'd shit my pants," you say.

Rudolph loses it. He smiles for the first time and pounds his fist on the table.

"See? That's a *real* laugh," you say, getting up from the table. "I'd rather drop dead than fake a laugh."

"Finally, a *real* comedian," Rudolph beams, staring at you.

You've cracked him. For the rest of the night, Rudolph is looser, chuckling freely at your jokes. He likes to be insulted, especially about his position of power.

"Thank you for coming tonight, Sauly," he says as you leave.

A few days later you cancel your golf club membership. Brisk walking is a lot cheaper than a country club.

"Bernstein," a soft voice calls to you in the locker room as you clean out your things. Rudolph stands there sipping a large glass of thick beer.

"Join me for lunch?"

"I'm off salt," you say, smacking the locker shut for the last time. "I'm tired of watching people eat burgers."

"Rodney used to make me laugh like you did," Rudolph says. "So I fixed him up. So did Jerry and Don. My job is to keep the world rolling in the aisles. Come by my office tomorrow. I might be able to squeeze another twenty years out of that ticker."

You never know where the schmooze will take you.

NEGOTIATING *101*

by HAROLD MAX, literary agent

I WOULDN'T NECESSARILY CALL negotiating an art, but it is a highly sophisticated form of schmoozing. It's a high-wire balancing act between power, tenacity, and charm, like manipulating without being manipulative. To be successful as an agent, you can't display too many of the well-documented poisonous agent qualities. Charm too hard and you become untrustworthy—no one wants to be known around town as "the guy who schmoozes people into a bed of bad deals." Too much tenacity and you're desperate; flex too much power and you're bound to develop enemies down the line.

Now, if I were hypothetically going to negotiate on the author's behalf for this book (Noah had the chutzpah to cold call me for this little essay), I would lean on charm as a negotiating tactic. A book like *The Old Jewish Men's Guide to* . . . I can't even remember the full name . . . is so outrageously unproven and speculative that one would have to be insane to try and overpower an editor to get a big advance.

This book will either go down as an absolute failure or rocket so high into the stratosphere that you'll forget the entire OJM ideology is even specific to Jewish men.

All I can say is, I better get a pair of those OJM speedsters for writing this, or at least a stupid T-shirt. I'm an XL. Good luck with the book, Rinsky.

Class Clowns

> "Behind every successful man is a woman; behind her is his wife."
>
> —GROUCHO MARX

Class Clowns commute between the city and the Borscht Belt armed only with their own ridiculousness. But don't worry, it's part of the schtick. No respect, no respect. Some Clowns wear the same old red tie while others show up with an obvious headpiece, speak with a Yiddish accent, hurl insults with a venomous snarl, hold a fat, unlit cigar, sport a bad stick-on goatee, bowl haircut, and sunglasses, and scream for no reason—or don't say anything at all.

Underneath all the rapid-fire jokes and one-liners, Class Clowns revel in their personal brand of misery but understand how to be just tolerable enough to maintain a half-decent career spanning multiple decades. That's not to say Class Clowns aren't known to can their managers, agents, accountants, and lawyers on a whim and then beg for them back the next day—it's common practice!

That's showbiz, baby. Agony is the motor that keeps the laughs coming. If you ain't crackin', these fellas ain't livin'. If it bends, it's funny; if it breaks, it's not. Humor is just another defense against the universe. The only truly anonymous donor is the guy who knocks up your daughter. I'm two with nature. My wife and I were happy for twenty years—then we met.

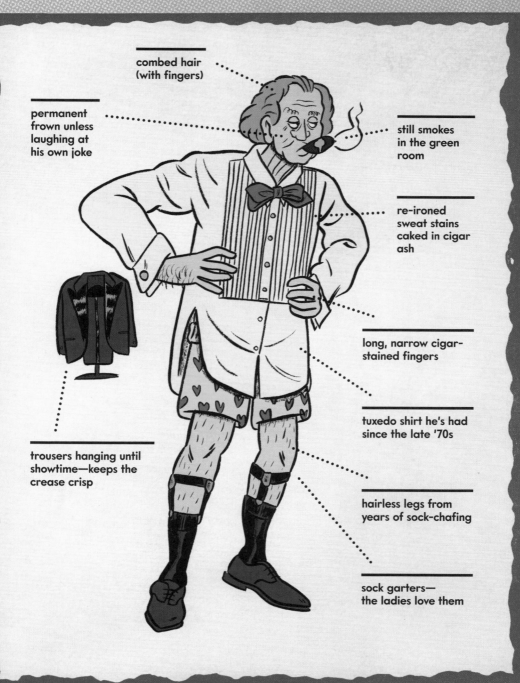

SOME CLASS CLOWN ONE-LINERS

RODNEY DANGERFIELD: "I haven't spoken to my wife in years—I didn't want to interrupt her."

JACKIE MASON: "I have enough money to last me the rest of my life. Unless I buy something."

GILBERT GOTTFRIED: "If someone else is paying for it, food just tastes a lot better."

LENNY BRUCE: "If Jesus had been killed twenty years ago, Catholic schoolchildren would be wearing little electric chairs around their necks instead of crosses."

GARRY SHANDLING: "My friends tell me I have an intimacy problem. But they don't really know me."

GROUCHO MARX: "Those are my principles, and if you don't like them . . . well, I have others."

DON RICKLES: "You don't have to call me 'sir' . . . King of All Jews is enough."

JACK BENNY: "Age is something that doesn't matter, unless you are a cheese. Age is strictly a case of mind over matter. If you don't mind, it doesn't matter."

JACKIE VERNON: "When I was born my father spent three weeks trying to find a loophole in my birth certificate."

ANDY KAUFMAN: "I never told a joke in my life."

JOAN RIVERS (HONORARY): "Life goes by fast. Enjoy it. Calm down. It's all funny. Next. Everyone gets so upset about the wrong things."

There's Always a Bill

OJM Class Clowns are fellas like your Uncle Mark who tell you the one about the husband who hands his wife a bottle of Tylenol and the wife says, "I don't have a headache," and the husband says, "Great, let's fuck!" For guys like Uncle Mark—not to mention others such as Rodney Dangerfield, Mel Brooks, Groucho Marx, Gilbert Gottfried, Woody Allen (oy), Jackie Mason, Lenny Bruce, and the primary care physician who says "don't forget to tip!" before ramming his Vaseline'd finger up your tuchus— it ain't all about cashing checks. In the minds of Class Clowns, when you've got the audience laughing, it's very difficult for them to bludgeon you to death. It's a typically Jewish disposition: the sinking feeling that the moment we stop entertaining, they start shooting.

OBIT by BAMBI MONTERO, *The Catskills Weekly*

MR. CLASS CLOWN WAS BORN IN

Sadzki, a shtetl in the Pale of Settlement, in 1917. His father, Chaim, worked as a ditchdigger in the mule cemetery, and his mother, Ahuva, was the maid of the local kasha smuggler. Mr. Class Clown's parents, grandparents, and thirteen siblings died of tuberculosis, and he traveled to America by hiding for weeks inside the boiler of a cargo ship. He first delighted audiences by making balloon animals on *The Ed Sullivan Show*.

"Insanity is hereditary; you get it from your children."
—Sam Levenson, comedian

CHAPTER 7

Runnin' the Family Circus

When all is said and done, the greatest joy in life is the grandkids—whom you appreciate infinitely more than your own children. The arrival of grand-offspring is the pickle on top of a life well lived. Nothing delights you quite like those little rugrats (and winning a long shot at the track). The greatest thing about them? They're too small to ask you to pay their mortgage, too weak to muscle you on the golf course, and too innocent to demand that you finance their latest, court-ordered rehab stint.

Whether you're the anal-retentive Hands-On Zayde or the free-rolling live-and-let-live type (see detailed zayde taxonomy below), the kiddos are the life-extending force that makes things exciting again. Aside from the new sauna you installed at your beach house, the little munchkins are what you care about most, and you'd do nearly anything to help them grow into half-decent people.

For whatever reason, schlepping across three states to watch your itsy-bitsy benchwarmers not play a minute in the Little League championships doesn't piss you off—neither does paying for their entire private school education. These things give you an unfamiliar sense of joy that you hadn't experienced until now.

What is it about their high voices, insane energy, and constant questions about the solar system (*Are planets made out of marbles? What's a Uranus?*) that makes you happy instead of furious? Why are you so invested in every aspect of their lives? Perhaps it's because they carry your name, and since everything in life is a competition, you want them to love and respect you more than anyone else in the entire world—especially their parents.

The HANDS-ON ZAYDE

THIS TYPE IS ALWAYS ready to do something with the youngsters. He's full-on grandpa, which means this fella has essentially transitioned back into being a kid himself. To become a Hands-On Zayde, you better be okay with spending a lot of time behind the wheel, because you'll be chauffeuring the kinderlach everywhere: baseball games, movies, ice cream parlors, Hebrew school, piano lessons, and juvenile detention centers. Since you've proven yourself a willing participant in your grandkids' lives, their parents (aka your kids) will take advantage and ask you to do absolutely everything, so buckle up.

The best thing about being the Hands-On Zayde is that the boychiks and girlchiks keep you young, and you've always got somewhere to be or something to do. Sure, you still trade a few stocks or work an odd job here and there, but it's the youngsters helping you stay occupied. Funny how much more you like being a grandfather than a father. It's probably all the candy— or the fact that it's hard to resent people under the age of five (but you're working on it).

Caution to the Wind

Since the Hands-On Zayde is basically a kiddo himself, he will be expected to eat like one, too. Despite all their good qualities, kids tend not to like smoked fish, kreplach soup, or leftover brisket. So when you pick them up from school, take them right to the nearest pizza shop, hamburger joint, or jelly bean store. Let their parents pay for the dental work (and Medicare for yours)!

"You don't ease into being a grandfather. It hits you like a sack of caca in the face, and there's no time to wipe it off. I chose to be an involved grandpa and I think that's why I'm still alive. That and the fact that I can still get it up once in a while. Thanks, Dr. Kaufman."

—*Sid Kloberman*, 87, retired bookie, on becoming a grandpa

**THE ECONOMY
CANDY STORE:**
**Five Bargain-Barrel
Sweets for the
Little Ones**

1

GOURMET
FRUIT
SLICES

2

BIT-O-HONEY

3

PEACH
RINGS

4

MARY
JANES

5

JUJUBES

Relax: You're not on the
hook for the dental bill.

Candy for All

Let the kiddos buy whatever they want on
your dime. At the end of the day, it's their
parents who will have to control them, not
you. Never mention the dangers of sugars
and cancer-causing chemical dyes. What
are you, a doctor? Who says there's no
nutrition in red dye 40? When you take the
youngsters for candy, they should be free
to stuff their little shopping baskets to the
brim. What does it cost you, fifty bucks?
C'mon, you made that much money last
night betting against the Knicks. Go Heat!

When the Youngsters Are at School

This is when you get a little moment to yourself. Since the wife wants nothing to do with you, and your kids have their own lives, it's just you, you, and you until it's time to pick up the youngsters from school. You spent your early days at Aqueduct University, so you still wake up every morning with a gambling itch to scratch.

Whenever there's an enticing race down at the track, you may tell your wife you're "going to the library to listen to an audiobook about the history of watch collecting" or "helping out at shul," but only you and the big guy upstairs know your true geotag. There's nothing quite like putting the grandkids' college money on a long shot. Afterward, if the kids ask why you smell like a chimney, tell them you saved someone from a burning building on 23rd Street. If they ask why you're broke, say you donated your gelt to the hospital. Either way, you're a hero.

The Holidays: Grease Fire Season

The holidays come fast, and a Hands-On Zayde is expected to know how to make a few dishes. Obviously, you never attempted to cook anything in the first sixty-five years of your time on this planet, but life is funny that way. This was a big transition for you, learning how to be in the kitchen for a reason other than snacking. No one is expecting your food to taste like Jacques Pépin's, but it should be edible at the very least. Pro tip: Add five times the recommended amount of salt.

Hands-On Zayde's Famous Chicken in a Bag

INGREDIENTS:

• A chicken, some potatoes . . . oy, just read the directions.

DIRECTIONS:

1. Crank the oven until it's pretty hot.

2. Take the chicken and dump tons of salt and other assorted seasonings on it. (Note: The more stems you add, the fancier it looks.)

3. Start cutting up the potatoes. Oops, you forgot to wash them—good thing dirt is full of flavor.

4. Dump pepper and whatever other crap is around the kitchen on the spuds (hopefully it's the same stuff you put on the chicken). What's that orange stuff? Eh, smells okay. Dab of this, dab of that . . .

5. Wrap the chicken and potatoes in tinfoil. Squeeze a little ketchup onto it if you wanna be fancy. Make sure they're wrapped up pretty tight, but it doesn't really matter. Remember, cooking isn't a science, it's about luck.

6. Throw it in the oven and keep it going for a while. Try not to fall asleep while it's roasting.

7. When you wake up, see if the chicken is cooked (or if the house has burned down). If it's done, serve it. If it's not, serve it anyway. There's nothing dangerous about eating undercooked chicken.

8. If all else fails, motor to the nearest Costco for a $4.99 rotisserie. The prices never change, and if they do, rally the troops. There'll be hell to pay.

The HANDS-OFF ZAYDE

UNLIKE THE HANDS-ON Zayde, the Hands-Off type prefers to stay in. They're tired and have too many things on their mind—like themselves—to spend all afternoon feeding and entertaining the grandkids. Ever heard of contemplating mortality? Can't they get a nanny or something? Why are their hands so sticky?

The bottom line is you've worked yourself to the bone for a little peace and quiet and have the heart attacks to prove it. You've spent half your life arguing in court, fighting the SEC about God knows what, and waking up at the crack of ass to put on a shirt and commute to the office, so you deserve to be left alone in your den to read the latest David McCullough and sip high-priced bourbon. You're basically a gentile, but the Jewish guilt kicks in when you hear that the little ones are coming over so you can't help but want to spend at least a *little* time with them. But you're not changing any diapers. Hope the kinderlach don't mind a little secondhand cigar smoke. It builds character.

HANDS-OFF GIFTS FOR THE GRANDKIDS

1. Gradient puzzle

2. Rummikub

3. Yo-yo

4. Rubik's Cube

5. *A History of the Federal Reserve, Volume 1: 1913–1951* by Allan H. Meltzer

6. 10,000-piece puzzle

7. Handful of Benadryl

A Generation of Morons

You're vocal about the grandkids not reading enough. All they do is peck at their phones, make a mess, and eat candy. They don't ask questions! When you were their age, you knew all the presidents and their birthplaces by heart (of course, there were only fifteen of them back then). By age ten, you had opinions about interest rates and thought the Federal Reserve should pivot to giving you more money. These kids probably don't even know how natural gas is transported between countries—when was the last time they went outside or read *The Grapes of Wrath*? They look like hell. They're pale and sniveling and always seem to have some sort of a sinus infection. Somebody get that kid a Kleenex and an attention span.

"If it was up to me, these kids would have a daily schedule; they should be tired from toiling. My childhood was spent picking up sticks and shoveling our neighbor's dog shit— it's just what you did. These kids can't hammer a nail. Their wrists are made out of glass. They can't do anything. Gun to my head? Yeah, I love them, sure."

—*Larry Yamnitz,* 87, retired estate lawyer, on raising grandkids

Bonding: It's Not So Bad After All

As much as you grumble about the grandkids, you pretend to like silence and solitude much more than you actually do. Even so, you refuse to indulge in time-wasting activities like Netflix, iPads, and all the other junk they're giving kids these days, so make your own rules. Since you're the Hands-Off Zayde who insists on teaching his grandkids how the backgammon cube works, the right way to stack a gin rummy hand, and the Benoni Defense, most of the grandkids aren't exactly thrilled about hanging out with you.

All that can change, however, with one little trick: Let them try bourbon. Give the youngsters a few small sips from your valuable booze collection and they'll love you forever. There's nothing like getting the middle-schoolers a little *shicker* and crushing them in gin rummy. By the time they sober up enough to understand why they keep losing their allowance to you, you'll already be asleep.

Grumpy Zayde's Flavorless Salmon and Brown Rice Recipe

INGREDIENTS:

- a few cups of water
- 12-ounce skinless salmon fillets
- Sliced asparagus (washed)
- 2 cups brown rice
- 1 cup spinach sliced into tiny strips
- ⅓ cup sodium-free chicken broth
- Salt (absolutely none)

DIRECTIONS:

Cook until completely flavorless.

The Will

**"He willed his body to science.
Science is contesting the will."**

—Henny Youngman

IN EVERY OLD JEWISH MAN'S life there comes a time when you have to start thinking about the end. Who gets your ancient, broken watch collection? Who gets the moldy, sweat-encrusted baseball hats? How about the Napoleonic-era paper clip stockpile? It's all about playing favorites. Sure, your daughter called you a lot on the phone, but you could never understand why she married that guy Steve. You're not crazy about funding that schmuck's early retirement. Your son never called you unless he needed a line of credit, but he carries your name, which unfortunately counts for something in this world. As King Solomon would say, it's a lose-lose.

There are so many factors to consider when drafting a will.

For some, your bequests are an opportunity to give back to worthy causes like charities, hospitals, the deli tab you never paid, and decaf coffee lobbyist groups. For others, a will is more like a ledger of all life's resentments. This is the healthier way to think about it. But the most painful thing is the realization that you won't be around to sample the spread at your own funeral.

Whatever kind of grandpa you are, it does make you happy to know that you'll be leaving behind both a full plate of sturgeon and a lifetime of memories for the entire family to cherish. As much of a pain as you were, you love your family and they loved you right back. Except for your second cousin Lenny Dervitzky. Screw that guy.

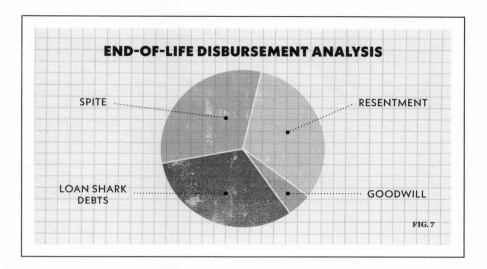

END-OF-LIFE DISBURSEMENT ANALYSIS

SPITE

RESENTMENT

LOAN SHARK DEBTS

GOODWILL

FIG. 7

DEATHBED REGRETS LIST

1. Buying extra low-fat cottage cheese in 1967—what was I thinking?

2. Passing on those Johnson & Johnson bonds when they tanked in 1981

3. Not making a move on Barbara Rappaport at the JCC formal

4. Pricey 50th wedding anniversary trip to Paris—could've stayed home

5. Laughing at Elliot Munchin's bad joke 16 years ago

6. Sticking my arm in that wood chipper

7. Going to the dentist

8. Purchasing home insurance

9. Hydrating

10. Buying the budget-option death bed

Woo-Woo Tarots

"Turns out, converting doesn't help you metabolize dairy."

—**BOB DYLAN,**
maybe

In their heyday, these fellas wrote songs, poems, and manifestos. They lived on the wellspring of creativity, hoping they'd never run out of juice. But everything fades, and Woo-Woo Tarot OJM hold onto the magic and legend of their youth with a death grip stronger than last week's peyote trip.

To become a Woo-Woo OJM, you'd better be busy being born, not busy dying—but that doesn't mean peddling cheap grade-school positivity. These guys never let go of their pain, hostility, and, more than anything, petty conflict. Despite fixating for hours in the Burmese meditation position on the crimes of the past—and getting their prostates removed two decades earlier—they manage to have kids well into their sixties. New young girlfriends and kids whose names they can't remember make them feel alive and hopeful again. After all, everything was better before—the music, the art, the painting, the poetry. Everything except the edibles.

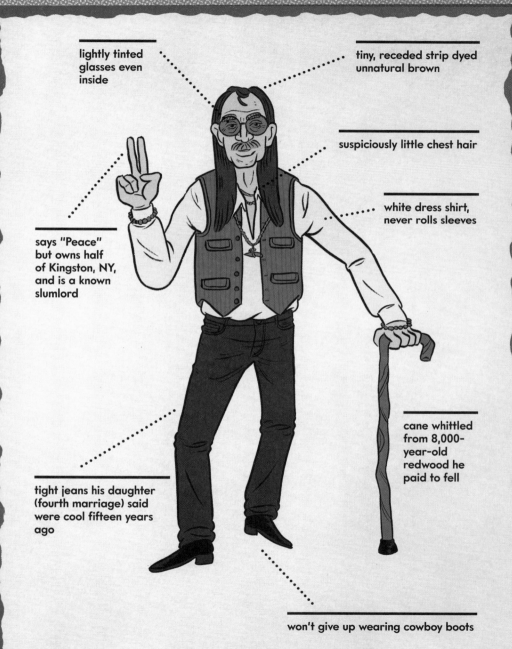

lightly tinted glasses even inside

tiny, receded strip dyed unnatural brown

suspiciously little chest hair

white dress shirt, never rolls sleeves

says "Peace" but owns half of Kingston, NY, and is a known slumlord

cane whittled from 8,000-year-old redwood he paid to fell

tight jeans his daughter (fourth marriage) said were cool fifteen years ago

won't give up wearing cowboy boots

Men of the Bead

If these Woo-Woos were once famous musicians, then these days they write poetry, garden, or cook. But they don't have the creative juice they once did and are all too aware of it. *Yesterday* is a painful muse, and they spend their adult lives trying to regain it, grasping at husks of lost inspired youth. "Remember when" may be the lowest form of conversation, but it's in these brief visions of yesteryear that the freedom of a bygone era keep the creaky wheels of Woo-Woo tumbling down a dusty road . . . or some shit.

Most of these fellas indulged heavily in their youth: drugs, protests, Joshua Tree, Woodstock, and hand jobs in the bathroom at the Bitter End, that kinda thing. But these days it's about sanding the edges of what was and wheezing through it.

"You start off irresistible. And then you become resistible. And then you become transparent—not exactly invisible, but as if you are seen through old plastic."

—Leonard Cohen, "Stages," 2013

Poetry Won't Pay the Child Support

Woo-Woo OJM spend a lot of time on the carpet listening to ocean sounds, picking sand from between their toes, taking nature walks, blending smoothies, joining co-ops, sitting cross-legged, or shooting wheatgrass. Many of them were smart with their dough and spent the last couple of decades living in the country, taking short trips to New York, London, and L.A. to sign autobiographies or talk about Joan Baez and Joan Didion or whoever is at the 92nd Street Y. Gotta stay relevant.

The more renowned a Woo-Woo used to be, the more estranged from their family members wherever they are now. These fellas know how to live on royalty checks and pay child support for the ten kids they've carelessly sired. But as your career fades and you ease your way into Woo-Woo OJM status, you'd better get used to a growing list of failed marriages, children and grandchildren you hardly know and have no clue how to parent, and European estates you don't visit.

OBIT by ARCHER C. MANDLEBAUM, *The Woodstock Daily*

WOO-WOO TAROT, WHO LEFT

behind a career as a respected accountant in Larchmont to join a Buddhist sect in Big Sur, chant words every day that he never learned to pronounce, smoke pot amid long coughing fits, play the triangle on a couple of as-yet-unreleased Leonard Cohen songs, and give life advice that would seriously mislead his wayward nephew during several family gatherings, died on Wednesday in Ojai, California, at a temple he was visiting to test out the fabric of the monks' robes before deciding whether he would join full time.

"My parents didn't want to move to Florida, but they turned sixty and that's the law."

—Jerry Seinfeld

CHAPTER 8

Hairy Old Men Like It Hot

Grab the tanning oil and throw on those wraparound shades—it's time to head for warmer climes. Since you're over the age of sixty, you need the kind of heat that melts phones and kills newborns and puppies when exposed for longer than ten minutes. Crank it up! Dump that Park Slope brownstone (don't worry, you should pocket around 5,000 percent of the original 1967 sale price) and jump a plane to Boca, Jupiter, or Zichron Yaakov.

Welcome to PARADISO

NOTHING'S PERFECT, but South Florida is pretty damn close. Despite baking in 105-degree heat most of the time, you will still feel a little chilly, so bring a brightly colored cardigan and get ready to head to your local sauna. If your driver's license has expired, don't worry about it. No one cares. At the end of the day, driving is basically just guessing. Crank the wheel this way or that and hope you get there without hitting anyone. Things have a way of working themselves out.

Remember, you're in paradise. In Florida there's sunshine, golf, tennis skirts, unlimited towels, palm trees, apricot sours as far as the eye can see, and hundreds of millions of Old Jewish Men. Stop futzing around in cold climates—that snow is no good for the heart. It's time to live out your days with some pizzazz, so fasten those Velcro sneaks and get ready to power walk to the early-bird special. And don't forget to smuggle out a few extra cheese Danishes in your pockets.

Gentlemen of Leisure

Just because you live in South Florida doesn't mean you don't need a vacation. OJM need a vacation from a vacation. Even if all you do is drink coffee, eat, and play golf, you could still use some time off, tout suite! Take a break from spouses, friends, grandkids, restaurants, lawyers, accountants, JCC pickleball pals, loan sharks, and proctologists. Well, maybe not the proctologist . . . that's your main man (and the best part of the week).

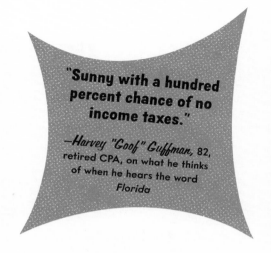

"Sunny with a hundred percent chance of no income taxes."

—Harvey "Goof" Guffman, 82, retired CPA, on what he thinks of when he hears the word Florida

Apricot Sour Recipe

INGREDIENTS

- 1 tiny drop apricot brandy
- 1 tiny drop sweet vermouth
- ½ pound sugar
- 3 ounces fresh lemon juice
- 1 large egg
- 3 dashes of orange bitters
- Ice (but not too much)
- 1 fresh apricot slice
- 1 brandied cherry
- Sweet tooth

DIRECTIONS

Pour the brandy, vermouth, sugar, lemon juice, egg, bitters, and ice in a cocktail shaker and shake well. Strain into an ice-filled rocks glass and garnish with the apricot slice and cherry. Take one sip, pass out the rest of the day from diabetic shock, and wake up three days later in hypoglycemic shock. Rinse and repeat. L'chaim.

The Joys of a Gated Community

There's nothing quite like armed guards and steel gates to lull you to sleep at night. As an Old Jewish Man, you can rest easy knowing that everyone is being kept far, far away from your well-protected abode. If friends, relatives, business acquaintances, or money lenders attempt to enter your gated community at an indecent hour—or any hour, for that matter—they'll be told you either died in your sleep last night or moved back to New York. That or they'll be confronted by a pack of rabid dogs (or worse, your wife). After all, this is your kingdom, and you deserve beauty sleep. Tomorrow is another big day of golf, slurping pulpy OJ in the sun, wolfing down high-fiber breakfast food, complaining about the air conditioner, shouting, and more golf. The same as yesterday!

> "There's two ways to back out of a driveway. Either you inch out very slowly and make sure no one's coming, or you close your eyes, press on the accelerator, and hope for the best."
>
> —*George Eisenberg*, 98, Pembroke Pines, Florida, retired golf ball salesman

Kickin' Up the Flippers

Being alive is exhausting and there's no time to do anything but relax. After all, you need to conserve energy for eating and drinking coffee until you fall asleep. To maximize relaxation time, make sure everyone leaves you the hell alone with no noise except the sound of the Marlins game purring on AM radio. This could be on the beach, next to a pool, or in the shvitz—just think of the possibilities.

But wherever you decide to kick back, you will always find something to complain about. *Maybe we should sit over there? Do you feel that freezing cold breeze?* An OJM needs the top umbrella spot and the most comfortable chair with just the right amount of shade. If there's a brand-new way to relax, you want in on it. If L.L.Bean just put out a beach chair with an ergonomically enhanced footrest and cupholder, or Lands' End has a new motorized rocking chair with a built-in air conditioner, *buy buy buy!*

FLORIDA STATS

OJM population north of Broward County: **0**

OJM population south of Broward County: **400 million**

Average dinner time: **1 p.m.**

Average bedtime: **3 p.m.**

Number of astronaut pens in South Florida: **5 million**
   (one for every household—they write upside down!)

Number of Old Jewish Women bragging that they sleep with
   the co-op board president every night: **8 million**

Percentage of OJM claiming to be co-op board president: **100**

Floral short-sleeved shirts per household: **200**

Green cardigans per household: **37**

Cadillacs per household: **6**

Full cottage cheese containers per refrigerator: **87**

Average cases of Fresca per household: **39**

Average home thermostat setting: **106°F**

Golf courses per square mile: **5,000**

Synagogues per square mile (that you refuse to go to): **22,500**

Percentage of residents over ninety years old with active driver's
   licenses: **100**

Average speed limit: **70 MPH**

Suggested speed limit: **5 MPH**

Hoarding Real Estate, the Cuban OJM Way

It's time to take a page out of the Cuban Old Jewish Man playbook and start buying up all the real estate in Little Havana. You may think that these OJM are the fellas all over Miami sitting outside playing dominos, smoking cigars, and yelling at each other—nah. Cuban OJM like to live under the radar and there's only about 1,500 left in the United States. Truth is, when you've got half the Gold Coast in your hairy palm, you don't gotta show the whole world how big your little mendal is.

It's better to keep things close to the vest—they don't even let their best friends or wives know how many strip malls they own in Miami-Dade. It's only when they kick the bucket and pass it to the next of kin that business partners and mistresses come out of the woodwork with lawsuits and threats, claiming ownership. If you're just getting started, find the absolute worst neighborhoods in South Florida and then do whatever you possibly can to put down a deposit. Make sure it's in your name, and don't tell a soul.

Old Jew and the Sea

IF YOU THINK THE BEACH IS the best place to relax, you're cooking the wrong side of the tuna, big fella. Hey, rookie—go to the pool! Swimming pools don't come with the millions of granules of sand you'll spend the next ten years picking out of your tuchus. Sand is the enemy— it'll get in your bed, your shoes, on the floor next to the toilet, and in your food. That extra crunch isn't supposed to be there, chief.

Dentists Are All Criminals

Dentists make a living on sand. If you ever bother listening to your dentist when they're yammering on while you've got a mouthful of metal, you'll notice how happy they are that you just got back from a beach vacation. Well, the jig is up. Dentists are what Old Jewish Men call "beach pumpers." They want all their clients to hit the beaches just so they can get sand in their food and ruin their teeth. It's all a racket. You're on to them.

Florida OJM Starter Pack

Tuchus-Watching for Beginners

The only thing that can get an Old Jewish Man to the beach is the promise of spotting a good tuchus, or as they say in the Old World, a "plumpkin tush." Ever wonder why OJM never seem to finish the books they take to the beach? A "beach read" is the hardcover you've been dragging around for the last thirty years and never read past the first page. You don't even know the title, but it's thick and makes you look smart. When people ask what it's about, you say, "life, death, intercourse . . . you know, the big stuff." But guess what: Grandpa Izzy's been reading *The History of the Piano String from E to F Sharp* for fourteen years because it's a useful cover for tuchus-watching.

Towels, Toilets, and Tuchus

If there's tuchus at the pool, you can lose the beach's number. There's a million ways to keel over and die at the beach, but pools are risk-free. Do you have any idea how many sand-related deaths occur each year? No one knows for sure, but it's probably a lot. More importantly, there's no complimentary towels or mint-basil lemon water at the beach, just bad parking and relentless heat. OJM flock to free towels like flies on horse crap. When it comes to finding the right *piscina*, don't mess around with a place that doesn't have towels, toilets, and tuchus. Oh, and coffee. Tea can be iced, but coffee cannot. Even if it's a thousand degrees outside, take your coffee hot with a shtickle of cream.

Gone Trying

In Florida, when you tell the missus you're going fishing for the day, she'll say, "You're not going fishing, you're going trying." It's not unheard of for an Old Jewish Man to dream of catching his dinner from a boat, but here's the honest truth: It just ain't gonna happen. Either way, bring Dramamine because you're sure to be sick all afternoon.

If you somehow don't spend the entire day hanging on to the railing ready to hurl chunks, retire to the cabin where you can take part in the activities in which you typically thrive: noshing, complaining about the captain and the size of the boat, playing gin, and hoarding all the cold seltzer. Leave reelin 'em in to the gentiles. It's good to throw 'em a bone once in a while.

IT WAS *THIS* BIG!

HOW TO SPOT *A Snowbird*

by JESSIE HEYMAN, *Vogue editor*

IF YOU'RE IN SOUTH FLORIDA from October to April, spotting a snowbird is like finding a sesame seed on an everything bagel. Or it's like searching for a silver Chai in a thicket of silvery chest hair, or a bald spot underneath a yarmulke. It's simple: All you have to do is look.

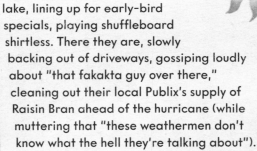

You'll know them when you see them, and you'll see them everywhere: power walking around the lake, lining up for early-bird specials, playing shuffleboard shirtless. There they are, slowly backing out of driveways, gossiping loudly about "that fakakta guy over there," cleaning out their local Publix's supply of Raisin Bran ahead of the hurricane (while muttering that "these weathermen don't know what the hell they're talking about").

If you encounter a snowbird up close, this is how it'll go: The male, usually in a synthetic golf polo and clip-on sunglasses, will tell you how rough-and-tumble Brooklyn was when he grew up. The female, wearing a chintzy patterned top and strong perfume, wants to show you pictures—usually of her grandchildren, but sometimes of a handsome nephew in Scarsdale, who is very successful and just *happens* to be single.

And when these snowbirds fly back north, South Florida becomes one giant empty nest. The line at the pharmacy shortens, the coveted accessible parking spots lie dormant. It just isn't right. It's like a bagel without the schmear, a pastrami on rye without the Alka-Seltzer . . .

BOCA

The City that Always Sleeps

COME BASK IN THE GLORY OF BOCA RATON: the most desirable place to die in the world. Every Old Jewish Man wants to be buried in the Kingdom of Boca, which means plot competition is cutthroat. It's never too early to start pushing and shoving and bribing your way to that dreamy final resting place. Once you do acquire your fantasy plot, showing off this piece of eternity will take you far in a lot of prestigious Boca circles. There's nothing quite like a huge stone at the Beth El Mausoleum or a full-spread package with a fantastic view at Fairway (who needs heaven when you're buried on a golf course?). It's like a vacation, except you're dead!

Boca Raton: the most desirable place to die in the world.

The Co-op Board: Running an Honest Campaign

Now that you've landed an enviable plot with a killer view that everyone hates you for, it's time to start campaigning for co-op board president. Armed with little more than an acerbic tongue, an argumentative personality, and a Machiavellian lust for domination, your election strategy is simple: character defamation, overpromising, ballot stuffing, lying about your experience, dividing and conquering, yada yada yada. You know the game. When they go high, you go low. When they go low, you go even lower. And just when they think you can't go any lower, you throw out your back. Remember, there's no such thing as morality in politics (or chiropractics).

Not-So-Benevolent Dictator

Congratulations on winning your election! Being co-op emperor means shouting down all opponents and vetoing other people's ideas during meetings. No matter how loud they yell, no one else has any influence or control over anything, so just keep raising your voice. Ruling with an iron fist means winning vicious arguments

---

TOP STONES

1. WISH I'D MADE MORE MONEY

2. HERE LIES THE WORLD'S BEST GOLFER

3. WHERE'S MY MAUSOLEUM?

4. DON'T TELL MY WIFE WHERE I AM

5. FINALLY STIFF!

6. NOW I KNOW AND YOU DON'T

7. WHY DID I WATCH MY SUGAR?

8. YOU'RE NEXT

THE OLD JEWISH MEN'S GUIDE

about important things: *No more salty pretzels in the game room! Glossy playing cards are now outlawed in gin rummy! Red is the better side of the Ping-Pong paddle!* This is your political career, so don't blow it—you gotta be cutthroat.

The main thing to remember is that even if you have zero interest in the topic at hand, get angry about absolutely everything. When in doubt, overreact. Accuse other board members of cheating, stealing, and subterfuge. Keep your enemies close and make sure to pass gas often and in their direction, but never apologize. Let them smell it—it's a power play. By implementing these strategies, you will scare, intimidate, and browbeat your way to reelection every year until you run the place into the ground.

NOTABLE BURIAL REVIEWS

"Great customer service. They picked up the phone ready to embalm and bury same day. Pretty good turnaround, terrible water fountains in the facilities. Will use again soon depending on who dies first—hopefully her."

—*Chaim Kohn*, 86

"Suing. This criminal enterprise has been using my payment information without my permission to buy a new hard candy dish."

—*Yankee Pearson*, 81

"Burial was fine. Complimentary mints or taffy would've been nice. It took over two weeks to receive remains and it feels lighter than expected."

—*Jacob Nemon*, 88

Tel Aviv

THE SECOND CITY

"It's like Boca with fewer Jews."

—King David, we think

SAY WHAT YOU WANT ABOUT the politics, the fighting, the corruption, the missiles, the this and that . . . at the end of the day, the people of Tel Aviv let you use their facilities without buying anything.

They've got bigger things to worry about than you hogging the can. In fact, most of the time you don't even need to ask a storekeeper, they'll just wave you right in, especially if you're old. Now that's livin'.

The Parliament

A Parliament is the group of four to six fellas you see yelling at each other on every street corner in Israel chain-smoking cigarettes, drinking sweet coffee or tea, and munching baklava. If the group has fewer than four Old Jewish Men, it's called a Swarm, and any more than six is a Public Safety Hazard. The Parliament is the sweet spot: four to six disputatious fellas with nothing to do on a Tuesday afternoon except argue, play backgammon, and ogle. It's what makes Tel Aviv so vibrant. People think it's beautiful tan people and tech innovation, but really it's secondhand smoke.

The Parliament, aka lifelong friends who argue all day and are determined to outlive one another.

Sitting Earns Respect

As an Old Jewish Man in Tel Aviv, you can stop worrying about being rushed out of a place. They'll let you kick around the cafés, restaurants, convenience shops (called *makolets*), falafel stands, and the backs of rug stores and spice shops for as long as you like. If you and a few of your pals want to drag plastic chairs over to the corner falafel shop, no one will say anything, even if you don't eat a single chickpea all day. It's a respect thing. When you get to a certain age, people in the Middle East simply expect you to become a freeloading, chain-smoking, argumentative fella—and they'll love you for it. Young people will even stand up to give you their seat on the bus. Best of all, you don't even need to say please or thank you.

Smoking, Shouting, and Turkish Coffee

The day isn't complete unless you've done all three in excess. The muddier the Turkish coffee, the more energy you'll have to smoke and argue about extremely important things like whether that's a real engagement ring on the waitress's finger. In these debates, it's best to find something that can be easily verified—whether the building across the street has always been there, for instance—and then claim the opposite. This way, when the other guys show you pictures on their ten-year-old flip phones that clearly disprove your point, you can shout "It isn't the same angle!" or "You can't trust phones!"

Once you've sufficiently fabricated stories and facts to make your claim, you can sit back, crack a bottle of Goldstar, and shrug while the rest of the Parliament yells at you. The more far-fetched your lies, the higher their blood pressure. After all, heart attacks are a badge of honor. If this sort of activity doesn't keep you entertained for an entire afternoon, make something else up. Say that the Pacific Ocean is man-made. Or at the very least, drill another espresso.

BEST NON-BEACH LOCALES TO GET SUNBURNED IN THE T.L.V.

1. **GORDON POOL**—great tuchus-watching; bring your own towel

2. **THE HILTON POOL**—sneak in through the back, or schmooze the doorman

3. **THE NORMAN POOL**—backslap your way into Tel Aviv's elite circles to get free entry

4. **ELITE SPORTS POOL AT TEL AVIV UNIVERSITY**—PRICEY

King of the Board: Shesh Besh

This variation of backgammon is where you earn real respect in the Parliament. Owning the shesh besh title is the ultimate form of validation for an OJM. The only time a Parliament isn't in direct conflict with itself is when they're gathered around the shesh besh board, waiting for someone to turn the cube. "DOUBLE HIM!" they'll shout in Hebrew. "You play like a scared cow!" they may scream. "Stop grazing!"

Of course, these long smoky afternoons throwing dice in the hot sun have little to do with winning or losing. Day after day, shekel after shekel, everyone ends up breaking even. Except Schlomi. He lost his house. And his oxen. Was that Ephraim I saw with his wife last week slurping at Shimon's Soup House?

"The sun rises here and sets over there. In between I may sell a rug, maybe two. That's life."

—*Avishay Naamat,* 85, retired rug store owner and native Tel Avivian, on the meaning of life

Tel Aviv OJM Starter Pack

Work Those Hips

If you're a local fella, Gordon Pool is your OJM hot spot, even though they're stingy with the towels. Sure, the membership is a little steep—you gotta bring your own bath wear and snacks, and it's crowded on the weekends—but they pump in fresh, life-extending cold water every Sunday morning. Pick out a lounge chair, down a cup of Turkish sludge, and spend the day sleeping in the sun. If you forget your towel, swipe someone else's—they'll be happy to help out an Old Jewish Man. No matter what people tell you about the beaches of Tel Aviv, forget it—the beach is for tourists, suckers, and thieves. The water is full of bacteria and empty Bamba bags. Oh, and there's sand.

Men of the Paddle

No matter how many sketchy real estate deals you pulled off last year, you're only as good as your latest performance in matkot (known stateside as kadima). No one cares if you developed half of that abominable Tel Aviv skyline, invented the cherry tomato, and charter private trips to Monaco to futz around the casino with your Bulgarian sidepiece—you still gotta hold your own in the matkot arena.

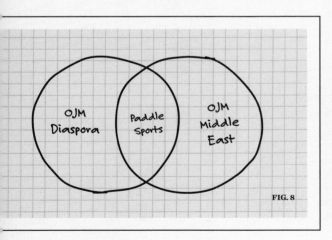

FIG. 8

At the end of the day, a challenger is a challenger, and when a friend calls you up to play on Shabbos, you can't say no. This is why OJM of the Middle East, despite their distended guts and lungs blackened from decades of chain-smoking, are still spry. But the greatest thing about matkot? You can't win . . . or lose. You simply hit it back and forth until one of you misses or gives up. Or has a heart attack. Shut up and serve, achi.

JERUSALEM

aka the Place You Always Hear About on the 6 O'Clock News

IF TEL AVIV IS ISRAEL'S second city, Jerusalem is Israel's loudest. The honking of horns, yelling on the street, and constant bickering over who speaks the most fluent Aramaic is enough to make anyone nuts.

Don't be fooled by the city's abrasive nature—it's instrumental to your experience. In fact, the bowel-wrenching daily strife is proven to be medically addicting. So much so, in fact, that there's an entire disease one can contract from spending too much time at the casino-like matrix of the shuk trying to get a better deal on a bag of sugared pecans. Remember, the first price is for tourists.

KNOW YOUR OJM JARGON

Jerusalem Syndrome: haggling with dried fruit and nut salesmen so much that you can't stop and begin waking up in the middle of the night in a sweat, arguing with yourself over the price of a single grain of rice

NOTES TO PUT IN THE WESTERN WALL

Please, G-d, let that shooting pain in the left side of my chest be muscular.

Make Jerome Powell cut interest this year by at least half a point so I can refinance the place in Palm Beach.

Forgive me for all the shrimp I ate all year, and this morning. I don't even know how I managed to find a breakfast buffet in Jerusalem with shrimp!

Just add a little extra oomph for Ginny the Dream at the Belmont next week. I don't ask for much, but she's 50-1.

Take my wife, please. Just do it. Now!

No Toilets in the Old City

Aside from a few nice views and the old stones, the Old City of Jerusalem is terrible. What's all the fighting about? Fort Lauderdale, now there's a place! In Jerusalem, everyone is out to sell you an overpriced Hebrew-lettered T-shirt. Thirty-eight shekels for fresh-squeezed orange juice? They better have squeezed a diamond into it! The only decent place to use the can is at the Western Wall, but it's a hike to get there from the Jaffa Gate, so forget it. If you absolutely need to unload in the Old City, run over to the Holy Bagel. (Tell 'em Noah sent you. It won't get you anything, but say it anyway.) Lousy bathroom situation aside, you may have heard that there are also a few places in the Old City of religious significance. Avoid them all, they're too crowded. Find a nice chair and sit.

Tunnels Shmunnels

Who cares about these so-called biblical tunnels? So what if they're ancient? What's so good about ancient? Ever heard of central air? There's plenty of ancient crap all over the world that isn't a thousand feet underground. How about Zabar's? It's been on the Upper West Side for four generations and you don't have to walk through a half-mile-deep basement to get there. The next time someone invites you to a tunnel, give them a history lesson of your own. If the riveting tale of Zabar's doesn't get their attention, tell them all about Fenway Park—it was built in 1912. You're not the only one with a history degree, pal.

Kosher Chinese

The Middle East is known for having some of the worst Chinese food in the world, but Jerusalem is particularly egregious. Israelis should stick to baba ghanoush and modern drip irrigation and stay the hell away from pastrami fried rice. Not only is Jerusalem's Chinese food horrendous, but it's also overpriced. A pile of crap should always go for market rate. No matter how physically ill you get from hummus and pita, don't get schnuckered by Elad's rubbery kung pao chicken, flavorless beef and broccoli, and soupy sweet-and-sour sauce. At some point during your time spent in the Holy Land you'll ask yourself, "How bad can it really be?" The answer is really, really bad. So horrible, in fact, that you won't want to take the leftovers home. If there was ever a sign, that's it.

The Meaning of Life

Most people spend their lives trying to figure out who the hell they are, what it's all about, or why AAA batteries are so expensive. The average shmoe has no idea why they were put on earth other than to eat, sleep, and futz around. Luckily, you're an Old Jewish Man, and OJM know exactly why they're here: for eating, sleeping, and futzing around (and you can complain too). So while everyone else is banging their fists against the Western Wall, praying to the fella upstairs and begging to know life's deeper purpose, you'll be sitting in the shade, double-fisting cigarettes, and slugging a cold, fresh-squeezed orange juice (that you haggled an hour for) with an all-too-satisfied expression on your face. That's right. Life is simple. Get one over on the fellas, eat some good meals, and smack the matkot ball around.

Hairy Old Men Like It Hot

The North Country
aka Hebrew Hick Town

THE FARTHER NORTH YOU get into Israel, the less the country will smell like shawarma and the more it'll stink of granola and patchouli oil. The north is home to a thriving community of Bohemian OJM. These are the free-spirit fellas who can't crack it in the big city anymore, so they move out to arid, mosquito-infested villages to live off goat's milk and wear the same pair of hand-me-down Teva sandals that are only a smidge older than the pebbles of Mount Sinai.

King of the Kibbutz

Northern Israel is much different from the rest of the country. While everyone else is worried about stuff like war and supreme court reform, you're focused on the important things: trying to squeeze more colostrum out of your cow's utter, glazing another jar for your sumac berry collection, and fundraising for a new bandanna. You're a northerner—all you care about is the little plot of disputed territory you've been looking after for six generations. You've spent your life toiling in the sun, but these days, milking the goats, trimming the grapevines, and picking olives is somebody's else's problem. Let the youngsters haul the milk buckets. The sun rises at your feet and sets over there behind all those trees and shit—now that's wisdom.

188

Eat Well, Crap Well

Everything you eat is pulled right out of the earth, and if it isn't, send it back! There are olives, cashews, almonds, pomegranates, fresh mangoes, and even camel's milk that you've personally watched being pumped straight from the animal's sac. Forget the Super Bowl—it's the best show around. As an Old Jewish Man of the Israeli north, you intend on literally living forever—the average age is 127.

So you'd better learn how to perform your own daily rectal exams and acupuncture and chug olive oil from the spigot like it's an Olympic sport. At night you oughta be drinking organic wine from Oren's vineyard and hallucinating on Ofek's famous magic mushrooms straight from the kibbutz. Some people may say you're overdoing it with all the health stuff, but the proof is in the toilet. After all, you wake up every morning to deliver a robust bowel movement that is the envy of every OJM in America. Who says the land ain't holy?

Basking in Your Own Glow

It's not enough to simply revel in that healthy, sunbaked Mediterranean reflection. Since every day is practically one magical tomato-picking excursion after another, it's your duty to tell everyone you know in America how great your life is and make subtle comments about how much longer you will live than them. (Also, if they ask, you definitely don't have a guest room.)

"Emm . . . compared to other men up here I am not so old. Around the corner from where I live is Moshe Bernaynu, he is 130 years and his wife is ninety-seven. She is young and sexy and when I go over there, Moshe looks at me, the young pisher that I am, and I see his eyes saying, 'Keep off my wife, you animal!'"

—*Ori Avni*, 88, retired bongo drummer, on his longevity

Hairy Old Men Like It Hot

Membership Revoked

You knew these guys back when they were minor sleazebags, decades before their mug shots were being auctioned off at Christie's. It was cute back in the day, their precocious schoolyard wheeling and dealing and spiking the punch at synagogue dances. But truth be told, they were always pretty damn slimy. Even on the playground they were rolling dice, corking stickball bats, reselling stolen baseball cards and lollipops, and intimidating kickball referees.

> "No one is going to run a benefit for the guy on Wall Street."

Unfortunately for the tribe, these fellas ended up making a big name for themselves in the worst possible ways. It's always the same pattern with Membership Revoked OJM. At first they do good things: build businesses, run for office, produce great movies, and bring honor and recognition to Jews worldwide. But the next thing you know, they're photographing their shvantz and sending it to every intern at NBC.

The OJM community doesn't recognize schmucks like Bernie Madoff and Harvey Weinstein as Old Jewish Men—they're no longer in the club. They swindled and abused their way into the doghouse for life. If you act like a disgusting bum, you get tossed out, simple as that. No matter how big you get it in life, you gotta play by the rules (unless you're a billionaire, of course).

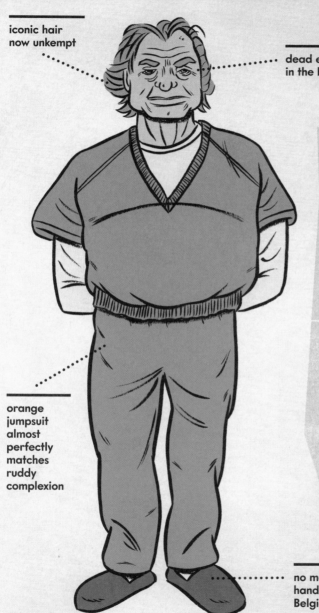

iconic hair
now unkempt

dead eyes perfected
in the boardroom

orange
jumpsuit
almost
perfectly
matches
ruddy
complexion

no more
handmade
Belgian loafers

OBIT by THE OFFICE OF
HORACE Z. FINKLESTEIN,
OJM Morality Bureau

MR. MEMBERSHIP REVOKED DIED DAYS BEFORE HIS SENTENCING,

when Sandy Koufax, Mel Brooks, Bob Dylan, Seymour Hersh, David Remnick, and Fred Wilpon——all investors entrapped in his Ponzi scheme—— formed a line at his table at Barney Greengrass and, one by one, spit on his gravlax, leading Mr. Membership Revoked to suffer a fatal stroke.

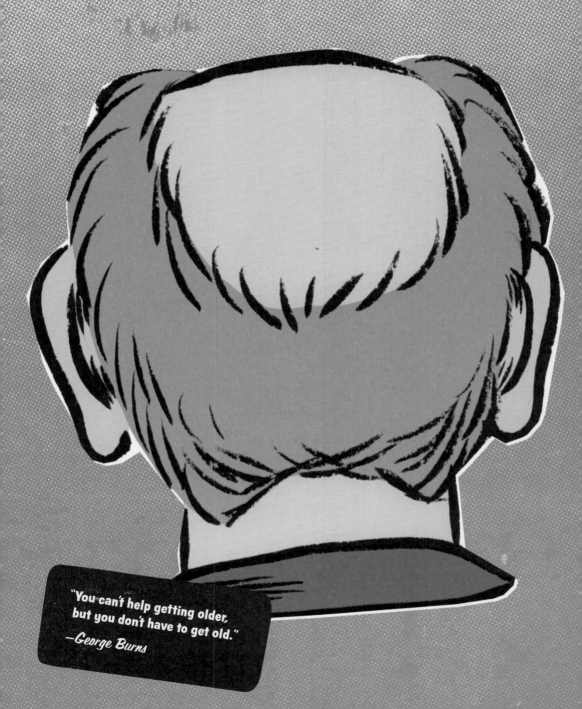

"You can't help getting older, but you don't have to get old."
—George Burns

The OJM Incoming Class

Every day all over the world, new wide-eyed trainees are inducted into the OJM Community. According to a certified board of well-educated scholars, scientists, and mathematicians (not to be confused with the Elders of Zion), fellas pass into OJM status based on a long list of complicated qualifications and equations. This highly detailed record of behavior, buying habits, gait, hunch, and other factors determines when a fella officially certifies. What you may not realize is that in the OJM Extended Universe, the harder you try, the less you get. So open up that newspaper, light a cigar, and sit back.

Acceptance Is Based On . . .

Hygiene (or lack thereof), pending lawsuits, number of divorces, daily nitrate intake, fashion sense (or lack thereof), manners, body shape, spending habits, Talmudic knowledge, musical ability, self-control around a spread, libido (or lack thereof), ability to stay awake for extended periods of time, coffee and seltzer consumption, reliance on pills to move bowels, dairy tolerance, ability to sit in a hot room for hours at a time, household handiness, and golf swing.

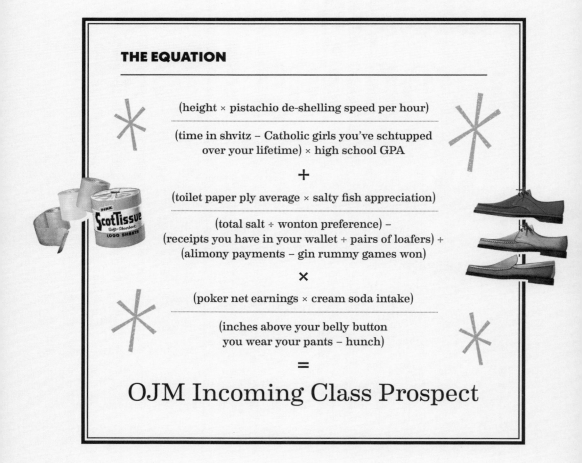

THE EQUATION

$$\frac{(\text{height} \times \text{pistachio de-shelling speed per hour})}{(\text{time in shvitz} - \text{Catholic girls you've schtupped over your lifetime}) \times \text{high school GPA}}$$

$$+$$

$$\frac{(\text{toilet paper ply average} \times \text{salty fish appreciation})}{(\text{total salt} \div \text{wonton preference}) - (\text{receipts you have in your wallet} + \text{pairs of loafers}) + (\text{alimony payments} - \text{gin rummy games won})}$$

$$\times$$

$$\frac{(\text{poker net earnings} \times \text{cream soda intake})}{(\text{inches above your belly button you wear your pants} - \text{hunch})}$$

$$=$$

OJM Incoming Class Prospect

OJM IN TRAINING

Still in Diapers

MENDY MURMELSTEIN: showing promising signs of indigestion after trying chopped liver for the first time

Primary School
• POTTY MASTERS •

ZEV PRINCE: sent back his eggs citing they were microwaved, not "cooked on a stove top"

HORACE GIMMELMAN: threatened to sue the family mohel for what he calls "a pretty crappy cut"

Middle School
• HOW'S THE HAFTORAH GOIN'? •

WILLIE DERWIN: hospitalized after what turned out to be "just another panic attack" during dodgeball

BRYAN REISBERG: spent hours at the dog park complaining about candy price inflation to any dog that would listen

HARVEY KIPNIS: purchased a single 30-year treasury bond for Liz Glissmeyer, most popular girl at school (still no dice)

Freshmen
• SPROUTS OF MANHOOD •

NICOLAS "THE KID" HELLER: pawned his bar mitzvah watch to finance a Knicks futures bet

AL TRAUBELMAN: sneezed so hard he threw out his back

Sophomores
• FUTURE SCHMOOZERS •

HERMAN MILF: in a legal battle with the neighborhood board after perpetrating "a snow shoveling monopoly"

LEW "BABY" BROWN: lost friends when he snuck into the cafeteria before lunch to hoard and resell ketchup packets

Juniors
• HERE COMES THE FACIAL HAIR •

HARRY GURNY: hospitalized minutes after grandfather took him to the sauna for the first time

ZELMAN GLICK: central figure behind three-card monte ring at Shwayder Summer Camp

BORIS YECK: self-proclaimed "cheese curdling" hobbyist, still single

Seniors
• BURGEONING SHOULDER HAIR •

JEREMY COHEN: chest hair made a full connection to his neck just yesterday

EVAN "HESHY" SHINNERSTEIN: the podiatrist says his hammertoe is developing nicely

ETHAN "MICKEY" LEVENSON: currently holding 128 extremely important receipts in his wallet

JASON MIZRAHI: threatened to sue local grocer for under-salting his rotisserie chicken

JONAH BROMWICH: elected by classmates as the most likely student to start an argument with the next person he sees

Super Seniors
• THE HUNCH COMETH •

BRYAN SEVERSKY: wears a heart monitor after getting too excited during most recent sexual encounter

JEREMY COLEMAN: fractured his finger pointing out flaws in his closest friends and family

RON LIEBER: currently fundraising for value-based grocery store, Boscoe, with plans to roll out $1.49 hot dog/soft drink combo and $4.98 rotisserie chicken

JESSE SCHEININERMAN: wrote a controversial post-doc thesis entitled "Everything Can Be Pickled," wherein he argued, "Why not?"

OJM Hollywood Scouting Report

WE HAVE OUR EYE ON SOME PRECOCIOUS stars showing early signs of talent. Also, it never hurts to put a few A-listers in a book about bupkis.

Maybe Next Year, Leo

The OJM Goyish Scouting Bureau has kept their eye on Leonardo DiCaprio. Do you have any idea how much crab butter Leo had to eat to look that good? But despite his rapid body hair growth and other impressive OJM-like qualities, it's hard to look past the thickness of his hair up top, or that he was somehow able to escape the clutches of Bar Refaeli, who is not only a supermodel, but also an Israeli. There's no chance in hell that a true-blue OJM fella could ever get out of that one. Eh, you can't win 'em all, Leo.

The Perfect OJM Body Award Goes to . . .

It's finally Joaquin Phoenix's year. About time the guy wins something. After twenty years of weight flip-flopping for roles no one's ever seen except *Gladiator*, Joaquin's body has finally settled into peak OJM form. In a word, it's perfect. He has what many OJM scholars and anthropometrics call "an enviable hunch." Joaquin's pecs have the ideal Jack Nicholson/Ben-Gurion-esque sag that so many men dream of. Close observers attribute his improvement to eating nightly bowls of Kozy Shack rice pudding, which might be the secret sauce. Surely there are other trade secrets Phoenix will take to the grave. But that won't be for another hundred years.

QUIZ: WHAT KIND OF FUTURE OJM ARE YOU?

☐ Scruffy   ☑ Clean-Shaven

☑ Pale   ☐ Tan (fake?)

☑ L.A.   ☐ New York

☐ Jewish Wife   ☑ Gentile Wife

☐ Chunky   ☑ Exercise Fanatic

CONGRATULATIONS!
You were born in 1976 to parents who work in Hollywood and now you're a successful director, actor, and producer.

Membership Withdrawn: Jeremy Piven

Piven had a great thing going. He was well on his way to being a favorite for the OJM Junior Doughnut Award, which is a big coup for potential OJM inductees. Everyone was excited about Piven's premature balding pattern—there was, according to the Greater OJM Board of Bald, "a lot of glisten." But years later, strange things began happening—all of a sudden the guy's got a full mop again. The Board gave him a formal notice that warned him of the violation, but Piven has clearly ignored it and he's pitching Extreme Hair Therapy for HairClub. What's next, shaving your chest?

⌐ Often Confused for Jewish but Not ⌐

JASON BIGGS · **SETH MEYERS** · **BRUCE SPRINGSTEEN** · **ADAM DRIVER**
BRADLEY COOPER · **STANLEY TUCCI** · **ELIJAH WOOD** · **NATHAN LANE**
ZACH LAVINE · **TARIK COHEN** · **EDDIE GOLDMAN** · **ALAN ALDA** · **NORMAN JEWISON**

Top Farm Team Prospect Hymie Schwartz

This eleven-year-old OJM sensation has been reading the *Wall Street Journal* since he was in diapers. Hymie wears oversized suits and sandals and rides the train like a pro. He understands bond yield fluctuations and will have a job at a boutique hedge fund by next summer. The ladies love Hymie, but he ain't interested—maybe next year when he has armpit hair.

Hymie's Daily Schedule

4 A.M.: Decaf espresso

4:30 A.M.: Workout: air squats, postural/balance exercises, running in place

5 A.M.: Bath (Hymie's mother doesn't want Hymie using the shower yet in case he slips and falls)

6 A.M.: Newspapers, journals, annual letters, quarterly cafeteria lunch reports

7 A.M.: Breakfast (two poached eggs, melon, cottage cheese) while listening to Bach, reading the sports section to be well rounded (go Mets)

8 A.M.–3:30 P.M.: School

4 P.M.: Chess club

5 P.M.: Backgammon club

6 P.M.: French class

7 P.M.: Russian lit

7:30 P.M.: Dinner

8 P.M.: Jeopardy!

9 P.M.: Bedtime (adolescent experimentation, aka self-exploration)

OJM in 2180

The future looks bright: bionic hairpieces, bifocals that don't slip down the nose, coffee that stays piping hot, a deep year-round tan (with no melanoma), and a self-contained odor that dissipates lines on the spot.

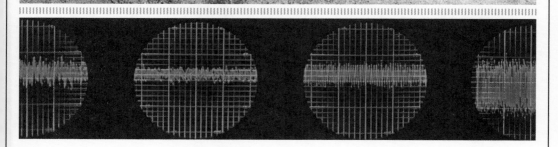

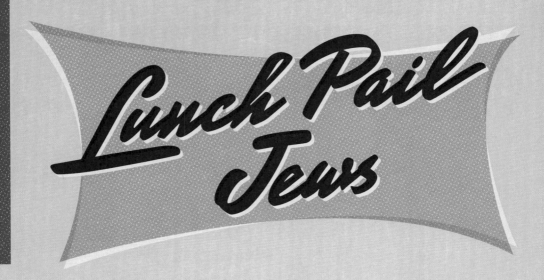

Lunch Pail Jews

"There's no social class among Jews. You're either lucky or unlucky."

These fellas brought their families to America in the late nineteenth century and found work as cobblers, flower salesmen, fishmongers, bricklayers, restroom and hotel attendants, street sweepers, garment factory workers, and tailors. They showed up feverish and penniless, a ghostly shade of pale or a coat of brown that Italians and Spanish mistook as their own . . . until the Yiddish spilled out of their mouths, of course. If they were lucky enough to gain entry into America, they stuffed their families into cholera-ridden, multifamily tenement sardine cans. Take what you can get.

Today, some Lunch Pail OJM live in gaudy two-family homes in Queens and work jobs not unlike their grandparents, copying keys and fixing shoes all over the city. They run plumbing and landscaping companies with their sons, repair TV screens, own delis and kosher coffee shops in Midtown, and rule with the same tough-as-nails demeanor. It might as well be 1905 because Lunch Pail types survive on the same mentality: work, and work hard. If you're employed by one of these guys, you'd better be ready to toil. Get yourself a hand towel.

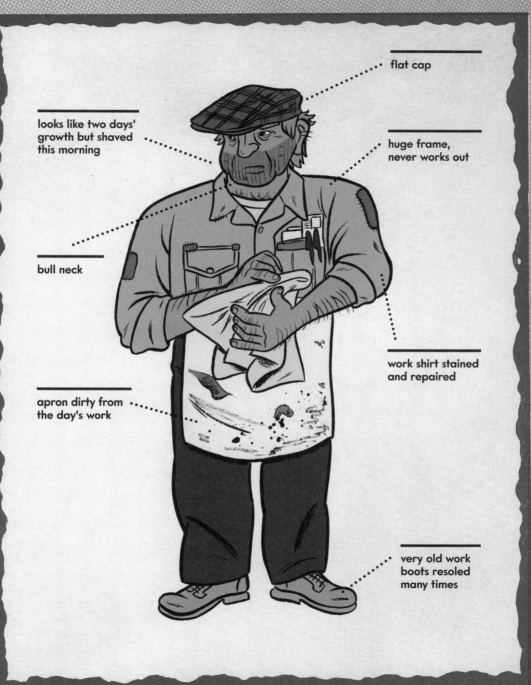

flat cap

looks like two days' growth but shaved this morning

huge frame, never works out

bull neck

work shirt stained and repaired

apron dirty from the day's work

very old work boots resoled many times

Last Follicle Standing

Lunch Pail OJM are known for their impressive ear and nose hair— shoulder sprouts too. Grooming is generally looked down upon in Lunch Pail circles. "Groom for whom?" they like to say. During midair skyscraper-construction lunch breaks, these greasy-handed, hard-boiled fellas are known to challenge each other to ear- and nose-hair competitions, which means sorting through forested face orifices to find the prizewinner. Every guy gets five picks, and whoever finds the longest follicle wins.

NOTABLE BODY HAIR LENGTHS

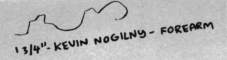
1 3/4"- KEVIN NOGILNY - FOREARM

1 1/8" (BOTH!) - ALFRED CAPLIN - NOSE

1 7/8"- ELI KATZ - SHOULDER

1 5/8". JAKOB KURTZBERG- KNUCKLE

19/16"- MILTON FINGER - FOREHEAD

Oy. Real Work.

When your days are filled with hard labor—fixing, reordering, stocking, hauling, scheduling—there's no time to shave. Lunch Pail OJM don't get a lot of breaks, so the weekend is shortened to Friday night poker. These fellas live to spend time with their families and rarely complain.

If their shops go under one day, they open a new business the next. They come from a generation of "doing what it takes" and haven't changed. They'll shovel shit, lay brick, or deliver newspapers to make ends meet for their hungry, crying kids— call 'em old-fashioned.

OBIT by MAXWELL SILVER, *New York Post*

MR. LUNCH PAIL DIED

from a kidney stone. He had survived a grisly child- hood accident involving a stickball, two bouts of lung cancer prompted by a lifelong cigar habit, assassination attempts at his union hall, pneumo- nia from staying outside to kibbitz on his stoop all winter, and stabbings by his wife and daughter, but once his time curled over the bowl no longer provided relief, he lost his will to live.

The FINAL WORD

(An OJM Always Gets One In!)

ONGRATULATIONS! YOU'VE MADE IT TO THE END of this mind-expanding treatise. You've learned to never wait in line, to wear your pants higher than you ever thought possible, and to take every opportunity to cheat at golf. (Sure, there were other things, but do we really need to recap them all?) You might say you've put a little hair on your upper arms, philosophically speaking—you're ready to become an OJM.

Welcome to a new and beautiful stage of existence. Despite all the kvetching, a sweetening has also taken place. It's the coagulation of the past, the final immovable act of a life well lived that has evolved beyond youthful longing, wanting nothing more than *to be*. It's not exactly the contraction of ego, but a new bloom on an old rose that sticks to its guns, leaves stool softener on the table, and lets long, gray nose hairs dangle loose, fraying in the wind . . .

You are who you are, and if you don't like what they say about you, who cares? If you're still young, ignore 'em, and if you're old, turn off the hearing aid. This is your life and you're the captain of this wayward sinking ship to nowhere—so fasten those New Balance 577vls! But the most important thing on this journey is to remember to buy the next OJM instructional guidebook. After all, anything that's half decent these days gets a sequel. Just look at the Old Testament.

One last question, now that you've finished the book: *Does it stay above the toilet bowl or go on the shelf?*

ACKNOWLEDGMENTS

It's surreal the way the OJM brand—or "lifestyle"—has caught on . . . regardless, I couldn't have made it happen without the help of so many people.

I'll deliver this somewhat chronologically: The early adopters of the account who, back in 2016 when it was little more than a few dozen skeptical fans, saw themselves in the fellas on East Broadway—I remain humbled by your passion. Friends like Devon Yesberger, who helped me identify OJM on Grand Street with his zoom lens. My early nerves were eased by Tommy Riefke and Caitlin Hurst on the morning of our first ever event, "Lox, Scotch, and Talk"—they helped me with filming, flyers, and schlepping gallons of pickles. Thanks, too, to Stanton Street Shul and Raskin's Fish for believing in us. Josh Seigel for being a constant force of productive realism and friendship. Gianni de Falco, for keeping me Mets *au courant*. Noah Segan for your uncurbable OJM enthusiasm. Jesse Scheinin and Maxx Loup, for the years of support in the fiction and arts departments. Cerise Zelenetz, an early OJM art visionary. Sam Deutsch, for keepin' us young and handsome at heart. Zev Prince, your TikTok skills are trumped only by your love and enthusiasm. Nicolas Heller and Mel Ottenberg for presenting OJM to the civilized world. The journalists who saw meaning in the OJM ideology—Jason Diamond, Lily Goldberg, Ben Blanchet, and Sophie Cannon. Marc Gerald and Leah Petrakis for helping me carve out a great proposal.

I'm grateful to everyone at Workman Publishing, especially my cranky but dedicated editor, Danny Cooper, who was spiritually aligned with this book, and Zach Greenwald, for his thoughtful encouragement and artistic openness. Also at Workman, many thanks to Lia Ronnen, Beth Levy, Suet Chong, Becky Terhune, Barbara Peragine, Erica Jimenez, and Ilana Gold. The extremely talented Raphael Geroni embraced and executed the design of this great lookin' book.

Every Jew needs an agent. I'm lucky to have Dan Milaschewski and the UTA armament. Robert Gatewood, my college writing professor—always your protégé—who told me to give writing a shot. Alex Traub, an obit scholar and future OJM completist. Jeremy Coleman and the entire Coleman family, for your enduring support and friendship. Suzy Weiss, my friend in all iterations . . . is this funny? Suz, what do you think? My pal, the only guy under seventy who can pull off a beret, *the* Dick Carroll, a mind reader and latke master. I couldn't have done it without Bryan Seversky, a fellow "sky," a warm, loyal friend and the most patient business partner a guy could ask for. Your brilliant design aesthetic helped make this book what it is.

The seventy-and-over club: Dave Roffe and the entire Roffe family, Aaron Cohen, Bob Terry, Elliot Satenstein, Dani Luv, Jackie Mason (bde), Ken Lerner, Tommy Stern, John Ordover, Jeff Stein, Billy Weeds, Arthur Finer, and all the OJM battalion who did or often didn't want me to take their picture.

This book is because of, and only rarely despite, the support of the entire Rinsky/Zimmerman clan. In loving memory of my late grandpas Howard Zimmerman and Irving Rinsky, Uncle Connie, Great-Grandpa Sam, Bernie Osofsky, Aunt Irene, Great-Grandma Syde, and Grandma Elaine. A special thanks to Uncle Mark, the family's comedic patriarch and foremost body humor expert. My best friend and brother, Ephraim, for showing me the way. My *very* forgiving wife, Liana. And finally, to my mother and father, Rita and Jeff. I couldn't have asked for more encouraging parents. I grew up in a house full of my mom's oil paintings and my dad's jazz piano. It's an honor being your son.

THE OLD JEWISH MEN'S GUIDE

IMAGE CREDITS

ALAMY: Pictorial Press p. 93 (Irving Berlin). **PEXELS:** Mart Production p. 128 (newspaper). **RAWPIXEL:** p. 183 (coffee). **SHUTTERSTOCK:** FashionStock.com p. 18 (Ralph Lauren); foto.grafs p. 21 (matches); Keith Homan p. 26 (Dramamine); Karkas p. 26 (coat); Rodion Kutsaiev p. 26 (pulse monitor); Arne Beruldsen p. 63 (MiraLAX); CKP1001 p. 63 (chopped liver); WithisanCH p. 63 (lox); Jill Battaglia p. 83 (book cover); lev radin p. 115 (Wayne Diamond); Aigars Reinholds p. 128 (cargo shorts); nopparada samrhubsuk p. 128 (bucket hat); Alexandr Vlassyuk p. 128 (sandal); masa44 p. 174 (towel); Real_life_photo p. 174 (cabana hat); Mariia Kurlova p. 183 (bald head); Debby Wong p. 197 (Ben Stiller). **WIKIMEDIA COMMONS:** David Shankbone p. 9 (Larry David); Urban Versis 32 p. 26 (nuts); El nomad p. 26 (radio); MorePix p. 26 (eye drops); Lkapit p. 63 (egg cream); Silar p. 63 (fish); Formulatehealth p. 128 (glucose monitor); Atomicbre p. 128 (earplugs); Mr Yukio p. 128 (battery); Fæ p. 128 (glasses case); Fir0002 p. 174 (cantaloupe); Jmustain p. 174 (golf bag); Missvain p. 174 (sunscreen); Elise240SX p. 174 (car); רפז-ה p. 183 (cigarettes); Amitie 10g p. 183 (lighter); Francis Flinch p. 183 (watch); Magnus Manske p. 183 (sandals).

About the
AUTHOR and ILLUSTRATOR

NOAH RINSKY is a fiction writer who occasionally sits in as the pianist for Rinsky Moonlight. You can usually find him loitering at his local coffee shop or hanging out at Costco. If he's not there, check the diner across the street or his Brooklyn home, where he lives with his wife and their mountain of OJM deadstock.

DICK CARROLL is an Australian cartoonist who specializes in autobiographical comics and fashion illustration (sometimes together, if you can imagine it). He lives in Queens with his wife, Sam, two cats, and a tiny human.

THE OLD JEWISH MEN'S GUIDE